HERONS AND EGRETS
OF THE WORLD
A Photographic Journey

HERONS AND EGRETS
OF THE WORLD

A Photographic Journey

James Hancock

Academic Press
San Diego London Boston New York
Sydney Tokyo Toronto

Text Copyright © 1999 Academic Press
Figures Copyright James Hancock
See also Picture Credits on p205

Academic Press
A Harcourt Science and Technology Company
24-28 Oval Road, London NW1 7DX, UK

AP Natural World is published by
Academic Press
525 B Street, Suite 1900 San Diego
California 92101-4495, USA

ISBN: 0-12-322725-9

A catalogue record for this book is available from the British Library

Typeset by Atlas Mediacom, Singapore
Colour Separation by Atlas Mediacom, Singapore
Printed in Singapore by MRM Graphic
99 00 01 02 MR 9 8 7 6 5 4 3 2 1

CONTENTS

Introduction   *7*

Classification   *8*

Herons and Egret species and sub-species   *11*

Hybridisation   *17*

Species Accounts   *18*

Individual Accounts   *21*

Picture Credits   *205*

Index   *206*

INTRODUCTION

In the Everglades National Park in Florida, visitors to the Anhinga trail are closely observed, often at quite short distances, by several species of heron. These we call 'people watchers'.

Having been a 'heron watcher' for more than 40 years, I have never quite understood why they do this. It has always seemed to me that their behavior is far more interesting than that of the human race. Such behavior is now well documented but, nevertheless, do not imagine that they always stick to the established pattern. We have recently learned that Green-backed Herons deliberately float bread or pellets on the water to lure fish to them. Grey Herons have been reported as catching small birds in flight like birds of prey.

Letters to journals and popular magazines complain that some activity seen by the writer 'does not seem to have been recorded in the literature!' Thank goodness this is the case.

My regret is that I do not have another 40 years of my life left in which to keep on 'watching herons'. Perhaps, however, it is just as well since the unremitting destruction of their habitat in so many parts of the world does not bode well for the future of these charismatic creatures.

CLASSIFICATION

I have included all the members of the heron and egret family. These include all the day herons of the subfamily Ardeinae, all the night herons, subfamily Nycticoracinae, and all the tiger herons, subfamily Tigrisomatinae. These total 47 species, although there are arguments as to whether some species should be 'split' or 'bulked'. The biggest argument is probably over the Little Egret, which here includes three races of white birds and three dimorphic races. Many consider the three dimorphic (or polymorphic) races, called Reef Herons, deserve to be recognized as individual species. In this book you have a good opportunity to examine them and see for yourself.

In the species list I have shown subspecies or races which are generally recognized, although in some the difference can be very slight indeed and often they cannot be separated in the field.

Should you wish to undertake a more detailed study of this family you should refer to *The Herons Handbook* (Hancock and Kushlan 1984) and *The Herons of the World* (Hancock and Elliot 1978).

The Whistling Heron and the Capped Heron each have their own separate genera. They are certainly day herons but are separate from each other, and from all other day herons. Not even the most avid 'bulker' has so far been able to find a reason for putting them together into a larger genus.

The genus *Ardea* is used to describe all the larger day herons and includes 10 species. Three species, the Grey, the Great Blue and the Cocoi, form a superspecies. Four other species, the Black-headed, the Malagasy, the Imperial and the Sumatran, also form a superspecies. This shows that within this 'super group' these species, although living far apart, are quite closely related. In the first superspecies, all are prospering, but in the large group only the Black-headed continues to thrive.

There are 13 species in the genus *Egretta* but with them comes much confusion. First, the Great White Egret of the Americas is often assigned to a different genus called *Casmerodius*. This is because it behaves more like one of the larger herons than the smaller egrets. To make things difficult, the other races of this species around the world behave more like egrets, and I have seen the race in the East perform a display which only egrets do. Perhaps they are different species even though they look very much alike? Second, some of those species put in *Egretta* are called herons, such as the Tricolored Heron. So here is more confusion.

The Australians became fed up with the whole business and put them all under *Ardea*. I do not think this helps. When the DNA analysis technique is perfected at the species level we shall perhaps be able to reach agreement, but knowing how things are, I doubt it.

Finally, the Snowy Egret and the Little Egret are considered superspecies. Now the recent invasion of the Snowy's territory has been achieved by the Little Egret, it remains to be seen what interaction, if any, will occur.

The Cattle Egret is given its own separate genus *Bubulcus*. Many attempts have been made to put it among the *Egrettas*, as its name might imply, or with the pond herons because of its size. To date, such attempts have not succeeded.

The pond herons come within the genus *Ardeola*, and four of them, the Indian, the Chinese, the Javan and the Malagasy, form a superspecies. All four look alike when not breeding, as indeed does the Squacco. The one that is very different is the Rufous-bellied because it does not change its plumage when breeding. When left alone they are highly confiding little herons. I watched a young boy in Goa kill one with his new air gun; this would have been impossible if this bird had been less trustful. Happily, in India at least, it is most unusual to see one harmed.

The Green-backed Heron has been described as three separate species, as one species, as it is here, or in innumerable species depending on where you live. Certainly, the amazingly different plumages in which this species is found around the world is quite unique. These varieties are all designed as cryptic disguises to prevent attack when they are feeding in the open and they are highly successful. By any measure this is a smart little bird.

The Agami Heron cannot be included in any genus other than its own. Its amazing shape and color are highly adapted to conceal it within its own ecological niche and to allow it to feed in its own inimitable way.

The night herons have two distinct genera: *Nycticorax,* where the bill is big and strong; and *Gorsachius,* a much more retiring group found in Asia and most having quite short, stubby bills. In the genus *Nycticorax,* the Yellow-crowned Night Heron is a highly specialized feeder and, because of this, appears to avoid interacting with the day herons. Indeed it will feed all day when conditions are benign.

The Black-crowned and its close relation, (another subspecies here) the Nankeen Night Heron, are much more aggressive but suffer continual attack from all sides when attempting to feed by day. This appears to have forced them over many centuries to feed at night. Their large eyes have developed to enable them to do this. The Asian species are not prospering but being crepuscular may be in better shape than we think.

The tiger herons must be considered as relic species and, although all five of them have much in common, they are so far apart geographically that they are given three separate genera. *Tigrisoma* contains three species from Central and South America. One species under the separate genus *Zonerodius* is found only in the New Guinea area and one *Tigriornis* survives in Africa. Very little detailed study has been made of tiger herons. I have spent some time with the commonest of the South American species *lineatum*. Where I found it, it lived in harmony with its surroundings and was not threatened by the local people. Elsewhere this may not be the case.

HERONS AND EGRET SPECIES AND SUBSPECIES

Apart from the nominate race, many species have well recognized subspecies (or races). These vary to a greater or lesser degree in size, appearance and behavior. They occupy different geographical areas or different ecological niches within these areas.

Size in relation to bills is usually a matter of food preference and the tougher the preferred prey, the larger and stronger the bill. In relationship to wingspan, if the bird flies on migration or dispersal then the wing is usually longer than if it is sedentary.

Appearance is most usually associated with habitat and the best example of this is the Green-backed Heron which dons a mantle of camouflage of whatever color blends into the surroundings in which it lives.

Behavior is beginning to be understood as varying often quite markedly between one subspecies and another. As the Nobel Prize winner Konrad Lorenz, a founder of the science of ethology, said: "It is dangerous to assume that the social behavior of one subspecies is necessarily the same as that of another living on the other side of the Atlantic." This warning is still not always heeded and often leads to confusion.

Syrigma

(1)　*Syrigma sibilatrix*　　　　　　　　Whistling Heron
　　　　　subspecies　*fostersmithi*

Pilherodius

(2)　*Pilherodius pileatus*　　　　　　　Capped Heron
　　　　　subspecies　None

Ardea

(3) *Ardea cinerea*   Grey Heron
     subspecies   *jouyi*
                  firasa
                  monicae

(4) *Ardea herodas*   Great Blue Heron
     subspecies   *occidentalis*
                  wardi
                  fannini
                  cognata

(5) *Ardea cocoi*   Cocoi Heron
     subspecies   None

(6) *Ardea pacifica*   White-necked Heron
     subspecies   None

(7) *Ardea melanocephala*   Black-headed Heron
     subspecies   None

(8) *Ardea humbloti*   Malagasy Heron
     subspecies   None

(9) *Ardea imperialis*   Imperial Heron
     subspecies   None

(10) *Ardea sumatrana*   Sumatran Heron
     subspecies   *mathewsi*

(11) *Ardea goliath*   Goliath Heron
     subspecies   None

(12) *Ardea purpurea*   Purple Heron
     subspecies   *manilensis*
                  madagascariensis

Egretta

(13) *Egretta alba*   Great White Egret
     subspecies   *egretta*
                  melanorhynchos
                  modesta

(14) *Egretta rufescens*   Reddish Egret
     subspecies   *dickeyi*

(15) *Egretta picata*   Pied Heron
     subspecies   None

(16) *Egretta vinaceigula*   Slaty Egret
     subspecies   None

(17) *Egretta ardesiaca*   Black Heron
     subspecies   None

(18) *Egretta tricolor*   Tricolored Heron
     subspecies   *ruficollis*

(19) *Egretta intermedia*   Intermediate Egret
     subspecies   *plumifera*
                     brachyrhyncha

(20) *Egretta novaehollandiae*   White-faced Heron
     subspecies   None

(21) *Egretta caerulea*   Little Blue Heron
     subspecies   None

(22) *Egretta thula*   Snowy Egret
     subspecies   *brewsteri*

23. *Egretta garzetta*   Little Egret
     subspecies   *immaculata*
                     nigripes
                     dimorpha
                     schistacea
                     gularis

(24) *Egretta eulophotes*   Swinhoeís Egret
     subspecies   None

(25) *Egretta sacra*   Eastern Reef Heron
     subspecies   *albolineata*

Bubulcus

(26) *Bubulcus ibis*   Cattle Egret
     subspecies   *coromandus*

Ardeola

(27) *Ardeola ralloides*   Squacco Heron
       subspecies   None

28) *Ardeola grayii*   Indian Pond Heron
       subspecies   None

(29) *Ardeola bacchus*   Chinese Pond Heron
       subspecies   None

(30) *Ardeola speciosa*   Javan Pond Heron
       subspecies   *continentalis*

(31) *Ardeola idae*   Malagasy Pond Heron
       subspecies   None

(32) *Ardeola rufiventris*   Rufous-bellied Heron
       subspecies   None

Butorides

(33) *Butorides striatus*   Green-backed Heron
       subspecies   30–34
       (virtually every country and many islands where this species exists has its own race and some have two)

Agamia

(34) *Agamia agami*   Agami Heron
       subspecies   None

Nycticorax

(35) *Nycticorax violaceus*   Yellow-crowned Night Heron
       subspecies   *cayennensis*
                         pauper
                         bancrofti
                         gravirostris
                         caliginis

(36) *Nycticorax nycticorax*   Black-crowned Night Heron
       subspecies   *hoactli*
                         obscurus
                         falklandicus

(37) *Nycticorax caledonicus*   Nankeen Night Heron
            subspecies   *manillensis*
                          mandibularis
                          hilli
                          pelewensis
(38) *Nycticorax leuconotus*   White-backed Night Heron
            subspecies   None

Gorsachius

(39) *Gorsachius magnificus*   White-eared Night Heron
            subspecies   None
(40) *Gorsachius goisagi*   Japanese Night Heron
            subspecies   None
(41) *Gorsachius melanolophus*   Malayan Night Heron
            subspecies   None

Cochlearius

(42) *Cochlearius cochlearius*   Boat-billed Heron
            subspecies   *zeledoni*
                          panamensis
                          phillipsi
                          ridgewayi

Tigrisoma

(43) *Tigrisoma mexicanum*   Bare-throated Tiger Heron
            subspecies   None
(44) *Tigrisoma fasciatum*   Fasciated Tiger Heron
            subspecies   *salmoni*
                          pallescens
(45) *Tigrisoma lineatum*   Rufescent Tiger Heron
            subspecies   *marmoratum*

Zonerodius

(46) *Zonerodius heliosylus*   New Guinea Tiger Heron
            subspecies   None

Tigriornis

(47)   *Tigriornis leucolophus*   White-crested Tiger Heron

subspecies   None

In many species of heron, lores, eyes, bill and legs change color during courtship, and remain like this for several days after pair-bonding is complete, and the first eggs are laid.

These are probably brought about as a result of pigment changes and increased vascularisation. Additionally, short flushes of color do sometimes occur as an indication of excitement (often brought on by aggression) and Snowy Egrets seem more prone to this behaviour than most other species.

HYBRIDIZATION

Hybrids are uncommon, nevertheless about 10% of the world's species have interbred.

In herons, such behavior is very rare in the wild, although commoner in zoos. Great White Egrets have hardly ever been reported as cross-breeding, but Grey Herons have mated with a Purple Heron in Spain and Hungary, and with a Little Egret in Belgium. One pair, of a male European Great White Egret (*Egretta alba alba*) and a female Grey Heron (*Ardea cinerea*), nested in a Grey Heron colony in the reed-beds on Lake Engura in Latvia. Four eggs were laid and all hatched, the young resembled the Grey Heron. Whether they will be fertile at maturity, only time will tell.

Great White Egret with Grey Heron and young at the nest in Latvia.

SPECIES ACCOUNTS

I have tried to give a short impression of each species in a few words. All herons and egrets have a great deal of charm and this gives each member of the family a character of its own.

Following this are the headings under which I give a brief account of each of the 47 birds. No attempt has been made to give anything other than a short summary. It is the photographs that are intended to speak for themselves. Some of these show a portrait of the bird, but many others show different types of behavior, as well as changes in appearance during the different phases of the bird's life.

I have seen and studied the majority of the world's egrets and herons in their natural habitats, but not all of them. There are, in fact, a very few species, that have hardly ever been seen in the wild, except over the barrel of a shotgun during the period when most museum collections were built up and of these we know little or nothing.

Identification

It is only in recent years that the importance of the so-called 'soft part' colors of this family has been recognized. In the past, detailed identification was thought to be reliable only when the bird was in the hand. This usually meant a museum skin. Indeed, even today there are many ornithologists who are loath to accept any other method of classification.

Two developments have occurred which challenge this concept. First, the use of the modern high-speed camera with long lenses has allowed birds to be captured in their natural colors and at different times of the year. Secondly, the use of DNA analysis, while not entirely satisfactory at species level, has begun to be accepted as an important method of identification and classification.

'Soft parts' consist of the bill, legs and feet, and added to them is the bare skin behind the bill called 'lores'. We now know that before breeding most species assume 'courtship' colors. These are often red, pink, blue or green and can be very bright. Invariably, these fade quite quickly, usually after eggs have been laid. This fading does not coincide with breeding plumage, which develops during the courtship phase, but can extend well beyond it.

While bright plumage is considered to be an attraction in starting the pair bond, such plumes are also used in aggressive behavior, as can be seen in the photographs in this book. Pair bonding does not depend entirely on the courtship plumage being adopted, and some immature birds will attempt to bond and often succeed. The success rate of such pairing is a matter of doubt.

The color of the bill, legs and feet is important not only in seasonal identification, it also helps to separate racially all white birds of the same species. I have shown this particularly with the world-wide-distributed Great White Egret and with the similar, though slightly smaller, Old World Intermediate Egret. Of course, separation at species level is also possible. An important example is the difference between the American Great White Egret and the white phase of the Great Blue Heron, which is often called the Great White Heron. The former has all black legs and feet, but the latter heron is longer and has light flesh-colored legs and feet.

Distribution, status and habitat conservation

The range of each species is generally known, although many birds disperse after breeding and can be seen as individuals or in small groups well away from their usual breeding or wintering areas.

The status of herons has and is receiving considerable study and a book giving population details on a global basis is in preparation.

Habitat conservation is cause for great concern. Both wetlands and forests, where most heron and egret species live, are under constant threat and all that can be said is that most conservation battles are being lost. If the human population continues to increase at its present rate, wildlife habitats will continue to shrink. That so many of this family of birds continue to exist, and in some areas prosper, is a triumph of adaptability.

Feeding

It is a fallacy that any heron or egret species can exist without water. It is true that species such as the Cattle Egret, and in Africa the Black-headed Heron, are mainly terrestrial feeders but at certain times, particularly when raising young, even they require food found only in water.

Behavioral ecologists formally describe observed behavior patterns in the scientific literature using initial capitals to distinguish these behaviors from general terms. Hence 'Foot Stir' denotes a stereotyped feeding behavior, rather than a general paddling about in the water. Likewise 'Standing' is a formal, erect posture adapted when searching for food, rather than merely as opposed to perching or flying. I have used these capital letters when applying such terms. It is clear, however, that because herons are so adaptable, they will often use quite different ways of capturing food and hardly any novel method can be ruled out.

Breeding

The most important factor in the survival of these species is their need to nest undisturbed. They will adapt to all types of habitat but the destruction of the nest, the robbing of eggs or the killing of young on a large scale will prove fatal.

Finally, I have only described Voice when this can be done with a single word e.g. 'boom'. Nearly all herons grunt and groan; to use a jumble of vowels and consonants to describe these seems to be of doubtful value.

1
WHISTLING HERON

Syrigma sibilatria

In the evening they flight in like ducks to gather at a roost beneath which they leap-frog over each other as they feed and quarrel before settling down in the trees. It is not surprising that the local people do not think that this unique bird is a heron at all.

Identification
Length: 53–61 cm (21–24 in)

Striking straw-colored neck feathers contrast with the black head from which fall narrow plumes. The rump, breast and flanks are pale yellow, and the back and wings are bluish-gray. The belly and tail are white. The bill is reddish with a black tip. The lores are violaceous, the iris is pale yellow and the legs greenish black. The immature bird is duller with streaks on the neck and lesser wing-coverts. The yellow plumage may well derive from the powder-down patches used in preening.

As its name suggests a whistling call is given in flight, and the young call to their parents with a harsh cry.

The southern race *sibilatrix* has pinkish-cinnamon wing coverts, while the northern race *fostersmithi* is smaller with a longer bill and the wings are honey-colored and less streaky.

Distribution, status and habitat conservation

The two well-separated races of this South American heron, inhabit open wet savannah. Patchily distributed in Columbia and Venezuela they appear to move with the seasons. In Bolivia, Paraguay, south-eastern Brazil, Uruguay and the Argentine south to Buenos Aires, they formerly migrated to the northern part of their territory but now appear all the year round, except in very dry weather. Trees are essential for nesting, so marshy areas near forests or, as in the Argentine, the remains of the forest are the ideal habitat.

Feeding

Whistling Herons feed territorially either singly or in pairs. Their diet varies from legless lizards, to eels, tadpoles, beetles and other invertebrates. Standing, Walking Slowly and occasionally Running after prey are the usual methods of feeding. They peck or thrust their bills forward.

Nesting

The flimsy stick nest in a tall tree seems inadequate to house the young, hatched from three to four pale blue eggs. When the young fly they still food-beg from the parents, raising their neck and crest feathers and hissing like geese.

Adults with raised crests in courtship display. The bright red bills have black tips.

Above:
Immature bird
feeding on insects.

Right:
Nonbreeding bird
with typical arched
neck.

Above Left:
Hissing/begging
food from parent.

Above:
Flying. Note the
duck-like flight
where the wings
never rise above the
horizontal.

Left:
Young birds in flimsy
stick nest.

2
CAPPED HERON

Pilherodius pileatus

This is another little-known heron which, like its neighbor the Whistling Heron, does not raise its wings above the horizontal in flight, but is described as 'parrot like' rather than 'duck like'. We know very little about its habits in the wild.

Identification

Length: 51–59 cm (20–23 in)

A largely white bird with a variable amount of very light reddy shading on the back and wings. It has a black cap and a white or grayish white forehead. Two or three thin white plumes grow from the nape. Its neck is noticeably thick. Bill, legs and feet are aquamarine blue.

During breeding the white plumage becomes suffused with a pale buff color, probably from the powder-down patches. The young lack head plumes and the crown is streaky. Only a brief croak is recorded.

Distribution, status and habitat conservation

This heron's range covers most of tropical South America but it is absent from the coastal regions of the west. It is an uncommon species that inhabits montane rainforests, feeds by ponds and streams and visits flooded rice-fields. Its shallow wing beats do not rise above the horizontal.

Feeding

This heron stands erect, then slowly extends its neck. It uses its foot to paddle and dip, and will sometimes swim. Its prey appears to be small fish, insects and their larvae, as well as frogs and tadpoles.

Breeding

Little is known of this heron's breeding behavior. In captivity, a dry twig nest was built in a tree and nestlings, covered in white down, were hatched from dull white eggs.

Above:
Feeding stance by river.

Right:
Captive bird showing prominent black cap, blue bill and lores.

Left:
Standing on a sand bank.

3
GREY HERON

Ardea cinerea

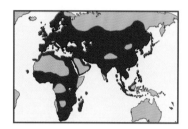

This large heron is doing very well all over the Old World (but does not visit Australia). This is surprising as it has been hunted with hawks, shot, persecuted by fisherman, poisoned by pesticides, and subjected to all manner of horrors man inflicts on birds that affect his interests. Its survival probably results from its ability to swallow nearly anything from an eel to a rat and to nest in the tallest tree it can find.

If you have a goldfish pond, then beware. A Grey Heron will clear it out before dawn one morning, and your expensive ornamental heron, sold to you on the basis that it would guard your pond, will prove to be a much-advertised myth.

Identification

Length: 90–98 cm (35–39 in)

This is the largest heron in Europe. It is gray with paler underparts. Its head and neck are white with black lines of plumes on the crown and neck. The neck and breast are streaked between the lines. The bill is yellow to dark brown and reddens during courtship. The pale to dark legs similarly flush pink or red. White neck and gray back plumes develop as the courtship period arrives. Southern and eastern races are paler and the race *monicae* is almost entirely white. Immature birds are a pale gray with few markings.

Distribution, status and habitat conservation

This heron is found throughout the Old World except in Australia; the most northerly breeding populations migrate south after the young are fledged. Birds of the year in particular disperse widely in all directions. A long-running census started by the British Trust for Ornithology in 1928 shows that numbers remain steady and that in some areas they are on the increase. Very cold weather, however, takes its toll on populations.

Their preferred habitat is shallow water either salt or fresh and they need four to five months frost-free. They will feed some way away from the water in dry grasslands. Most races use trees for nesting and roosting, but southern-most races, such as *monicae*, inhabit flat coastlines.

Feeding

With such a wide diet, all types of feeding are used from Standing, Walking Slowly, Running, Swimming, Diving and Plunging. The powerful bill is thrust forward to capture prey, whether fish, amphibians, small mammals, reptiles, insects or small birds. Where food is abundant they will feed in groups. They have learned to congregate at fish farms, bird parks and zoos, and at any spot where food is readily available. As solitary feeders, they prefer to feed at dawn or dusk and are extremely wary. They will scavenge and even follow the plough when the opportunity arises.

Breeding

Colonial nesting is preceded by courtship displays. Following a yelping Advertising Call on arrival at the chosen nest-site, plumes are erected for the Stretch display, Wing Flapping and Bill Clappering.

They are early nesters throughout their range. The nest is often flimsy and holds from three to five greenish blue eggs. It is built in tall trees when they are available, although reedbeds, bushes, walls or even the bare ground can be used.

Left:
Adult in nonbreeding plumage.

Below Left:
Breeding adult holding fish.

Below Right:
The eastern race *jouyi* is paler. The legs are flush pink after courtship.

Right:
Immature bird
resting in typical
stance.

Below:
Eastern race at nest
site with cormorants.

4
GREAT BLUE HERON

Ardea herodius

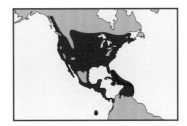

Like so many of the world's herons, this great species can be confiding, indeed bold, as it is in Florida where it steals bait from the fisherman's bucket, or as shy and elusive as it is in its wintering grounds in Trinidad where hunters abound.

Identification

Length: 97–137 cm (38–54 in)

The Great Blue Heron is a large dark-gray bird with a white crown, cheeks and throat. A black stripe on the side of the crown merges into a long occipital crest. The neck is gray with a violaceous tinge on the back and sides, and is striped black-and-white below. The back is blue-gray, the sides blackish and the belly gray-and-white striped. The thigh feathers are a distinctive chestnut. The bill is yellow with a dusky culmea and the legs greenish-brown. The all-white form has pale cream-yellow legs and blue lores.

An intermediate form known as 'Wurdemann's Heron' is a pale form of the Great Blue. During breeding, plumes cover the back and neck, the iris reddens, the lores turn lime-green and the legs become bright orange-pink.

Distribution, status and habitat conservation

Great Blue Herons breed throughout North and Central America, the Caribbean, Greater Antilles and the Galapagos Islands. There are several races, with the all-white *occidentalis* found only in small numbers in Florida and parts of the Caribbean.

In North America most races which nest in the north are migrants, with the exception of the smaller, darker race *fannini* found all year round on the Pacific North-West Coast. Southern races are much more sedentary.

After breeding, many individuals disperse widely reaching Newfoundland and even Greenland. Others visit Cuba and some reach South America; these mostly immature birds of the year suffer heavy losses at this time.

This heron is found on rivers and streams, in marshes and swamps. It inhabits shorelines, mangroves and tidal flats. The white form is almost always found in a marine habitat, but most other races move to take advantage of variable food resources.

Feeding

This species feeds by day or night in fresh or salt water. It feeds by Standing or Walking Slowly, often wading in quite deep water. Alternatively, it will Flycatch, Probe, Peck, Run, Hop, Wing Flick, indeed perform widely different methods of catching its prey, depending on how active and what size it is.

Breeding

The nest is a large platform of sticks placed either in tall trees in the north, or more often in mangrove bushes, in the south of its range. These are usually in colonies, but quite frequently solitary nests are found and some even on the ground. The courtship displays are spectacular and highly variable. Wing Preen, Circle Flight, Twig Shake, and Fluffed Neck, Upright, Arched Neck, and Forward aggressive displays are performed after pairing Bill Clappering. The eggs are pale blue and clutches of between three and seven are laid.

Above Left:
Nonbreeding adult .

Above Right:
With young at the
nest in a mixed
colony.

Left:
Adult bird in the
Everglades, Florida.

Right:

Growing young
begging food.

Below:

An immature bird in
its first year.

Left:
The race *occidentalis*.
An all white bird
found in south
Florida, USA.

Below:
Sometimes still
called the Great
White Heron. Its legs
are pale (not black
like the egret).

Above:
Breeding between dark and white birds results in a white - necked bird often called Wurdemann's heron.

Right:
The race *wardii* of Florida is a handsome bird.

5
COCOI HERON

Ardea cocoi

Why the South Americans call this heron 'Garza mora' is difficult to understand. Its only 'mora' (or black) is on its head and breast. Indeed its neck, which is white, is more often used to describe it in English but, since there is a heron in Australia of this name we stick to 'cocoi', which was first used in 1648.

Identification

Length: 97–127 cm (38–50 in)

This bird has gray upperparts, pale to white, on the wing coverts and tips of the scapulars. In contrast, flight feathers are black and there are similar patches on either side of the lower breast and belly. The neck is markedly white and the black crown comes well down onto the face below the eye. The iris is yellow, as is the bill, although it can have a dull base. Legs and feet are blackish.

The courtship plumage is quite spectacular. The plumage brightens and the yellow on the bill assumes a strong red tinge. The dark legs flush pink.

Immature birds are duller and streaked.

Like its superspecies representatives, the Grey and Great Blue Herons, it has a harsh croak but somewhat higher in tone than the other two.

Distribution, status and habitat conservation

This is a South American species found throughout the continent, except in the Andes, although not found south of Aisén in Chile and Chabut in the Argentine.

It disperses widely after breeding as far as the Falkland Islands, with one found in mid-Atlantic on Gough Island. Northwards it visits the islands of the Caribbean. Immature birds visit Trinidad regularly and I have seen mature adults on Tobago. It is found by lakes, rivers, marshland and even small streams.

Feeding

It is the least known of the three 'Grey' herons; it probably has a similar diet to the other two and uses the same Standing technique, as well as Walking Slowly and Head Tilting. It certainly eats fish, frogs and the larvae of aquatic insects but may well feed on reptiles and small mammals both during the day and at night.

Breeding

This heron usually nests in trees but I did visit a colony in tall reeds in the Argentine. Large deep nests are built and usually three sky-blue eggs are laid. Chicks have contrasting dark downy heads and pale necks.

This South American heron has a white neck but should not be confused with the Australian species of this name.

Above:
The startlingly bright colors of a bird in full courtship condition.

Left:
A rare visitor to Tobago, an island to the north of Venezuela.

6
WHITE-NECKED HERON

Ardea pacifica

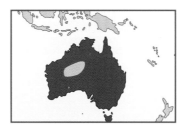

Just as the Australian aborigines go 'walk-about', so it appears that this very Australian bird goes 'fly-about'. Whenever and wherever rain occurs, in the changeable weather pattern of this country, a few of this nomadic heron will appear, only to move on when 'the dry' starts again.

Identification

Length: variable, 76–107 cm (30–42 in)

A distinctive white neck and a dark slate gray body and wings make this heron easy to recognize. In nonbreeding plumage these colors are duller and the foreneck has black spotting.

Soft-part colors, as is usual, change as breeding plumes are developed. The yellow of the iris deepens. Bill and legs are black, although the latter sometimes have a yellowish tinge, usually on the tarsus. The dark lores brighten to a yellowish green, sometimes blue. For a time the dark body and wings acquire a chestnut maroon on the scapulars.

Distribution, status and habitat conservation

The White-necked Heron nests throughout Australia, as well as in Tasmania and the Bass Strait Islands. Where rainfall is reliable, it is comparatively sedentary but it moves nomadically, often in large groups, to areas where wet conditions occur spasmodically.

Regular migration also occurs and these movements again coincide with the pattern of 'wet' and 'dry' spells.

It prefers open wet grasslands, swamps, lagoons and water-holes.

Feeding

The White-necked Heron uses many of the techniques of the *Egretta* species, including Foot Raking and Wing Flicking. It uses Standing and Walking Slowly methods from Upright or Crouched positions.

Prey consists of fish, frogs, newts, mollusks and aquatic insects. Small reptiles are also eaten.

Breeding

This heron is usually a colonial nester, often with a variety of other species. Some claim it nests solitarily, but only rare instances are recorded. A bulky nest of twigs and sticks is built either in a tall tree or in dead trees standing in water. Up to five eggs, usually oval and pale grayish blue, are laid. Downy young have gray brown upperparts with white head and neck.

This bird flies north after breeding.

An adult nonbreeder.

7

BLACK-HEADED HERON

Ardea melanocephala

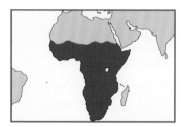

This is the heron you see first when you land at an airport in most parts of Africa south of the equator. It feeds in grass, and while it will get its feet wet, it draws the line at wading.

Identification

Length: *c*. 92 cm (36 in)

This heron is a black, gray and white bird, with three lanceolate plumes on the nape. The black head is offset by the white chin and throat. The lower throat is a distinctively speckled black and white and this merges into gray on the neck. Bill and legs are black, although the lower mandible can be a dusky yellow.

The yellow iris turns red during courtship with little change to bill and legs. It utters a variety of growls and grunts, mostly at the nest.

Distribution, status and habitat conservation

The Black-headed Heron is found throughout the African continent south of the Sahara. Migration takes place when dry conditions occur.

It inhabits open country, using dry grasslands where water is close at hand, but preferring wet meadows, ponds or flooded areas.

Feeding

This species stalks in a stately manner through grasslands, often high stepping with head leaning backwards.

All the usual species found in such habitats are eaten, ranging from worms, crickets, grasshoppers and scorpions, to all small mammals, reptiles, young birds and insects.

Breeding

The twig nest is flimsy and placed high in a tree, but sometimes in reedbeds. Two to four pale greenish-blue eggs are laid. Up to 200 pairs occur in some large colonies, but more often small mixed breeding groups are preferred.

The courtship ritual of this elegant bird is quite spectacular with Crest Raising, Stretch displays, Fluffed Neck displays and Bill Clappering, followed by caressing of the partner's back and flank with the bill closed. Considerable noise occurs with raucous cries exchanged.

Trees are used for roosting and nesting but most time is spent on the ground.

Left:
A terrestrial feeder on insects and amphibians, as well as small birds and mammals.

Below Left:
An adult in long grass.

Below Right:
An immature bird. At this age they will pick up any object they find.

8
MALAGASY HERON
Ardea humbloti

This somber-looking bird is very rare even in its island retreats. It may survive if enough patches of trees remain in which to nest. Only the forest areas that come under a local taboo can be sure of remaining untouched on this rapidly developing island group.

Identification

Length: c. 100 cm (39 in)

A dull mauvish-gray body, lighter neck and black crown describe this solitary bird. The bill, legs and feet are dull yellow, as is the iris. Presumably, some brightening occurs during courtship and breeding but this has not been described.

Distribution, status and habitat conservation

This Madagascan species is under enormous pressure on this developing island. It has been seen in the north-west and the central plain. Recent sightings confirm its presence on the Comoro Islands, although it may be only a vagrant there. It visited rice-fields and mangrove belts along the coastline as well as freshwater lakes.

— Never very common, this large heron is certainly at risk in such conditions.

Feeding

Said to be remarkably tame when Standing motionless, this heron catches quite large fish which appear to be its main diet, although eels and smaller fish are also taken.

Breeding

The Malagasy Heron normally builds its nest in a group of trees, but these require protection. This is offered by local taboos in a few areas but elsewhere it suffers from human predation as does most wildlife on this island.

The extensive development that has taken place has resulted in previously inaccessible areas being now much more easily reached. One nest was found in corralline rock well hidden under creeping vegetation, and this may indicate the problems that this species has in finding a safe place to breed.

This rare island heron is under severe threat.

9
IMPERIAL HERON

Ardea imperialis

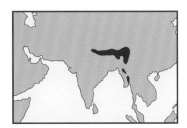

This second largest of all herons is having a struggle to survive. Its main problem appears to be wandering tribesmen who live off the 'fruit of the forest'. Large-scale drainage and timber felling have reduced the former impenetrable forest and thick elephant grass which grew beneath the Himalayas. Nomadic peoples now travel more, especially since there are now fewer tigers which were once a real deterrent.

Identification

Length: 127 cm (50 in)

Darker plumed than the Malagasy Heron, this highly elusive species has dull brown tinged upperparts, with its neck gray and crown somewhat darker, and a short pale nuchal crest. Only the chin and the underparts are white, although the wing lining also shows some white contrasting with gray in flight.

The iris is yellow and the bill dull yellowish green. The legs are a dark gray. These colors presumably brighten up if anyone was ever fortunate enough to see an individual in courtship display.

Distribution, status and habitat conservation

Found in the foothills of the Himalayas, Bhutan and Assam as well as northern Burma, this heron's range has suffered from habitat destruction and, over much of its breeding area, years of warfare. Although there are a few post-war records, these are as rare as the bird itself appears to be.

Feeding

One can only surmise that the diet of this species mirrors that of the other large herons.

Breeding

Few nests have been recorded. Eggs of greenish blue color were discovered in a huge stick nest in a tall tree in the Arakan. During the war against Japan a few such structures were noted but not, for obvious reasons, investigated.

This rare heron has hardly, if ever, been seen in recent years and is believed to be seriously endangered.

10
SUMATRAN HERON

Ardea sumatrana

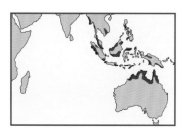

This most widespread of the larger herons has a plumage which is designed to avoid attention. Whenever I have seen it, the bird did not fly off but calmly walked back into the thick mangrove out of sight. If you find a nest, be prepared for a very loud boom of protest from its nearby owner.

Identification

Length: 115 cm (45 in)

This somewhat dully-plumed large heron completes the trio of these species in Asia. It is brownish-gray with sooty-gray wings. Immmature birds are more rusty brown than the adults.

At the time of breeding whitish tips develop on the plumes of the nape, scapulars and upper breast. The center of the breast and the chin also become white. Bill, legs and feet are a dull yellowish brown, but brighten up during breeding.

Courtship colors in the soft parts appear to vary, probably reflecting racial differences. The dull greenish-brown lores become more yellow and a male was recorded as having bluish-gray facial skin. The bill undoubtedly changes to a blacker coloration with some yellow on the lower mandible.

Distribution, status and habitat conservation

This is a much more widespread species than other herons of its size. Its range stretches from Burma, along the coasts of Thailand, through Indonesia to as far as the tropical coastlands of Northern Australia. In Northern Australia it is under less pressure from the human race than in Asia where, in most places, all wildlife and its habitat are being systematically, destroyed.

Mainly a sedentary species this heron lives in coastal mangrove stands, mudflats and creeks, although in the few Malayan Islands where it still exists, it is found along rocky shorelines.

Feeding

This heron is a solitary feeder; it eats fish and the massive bill enables it to crack open crabs and mollusks with ease.

Breeding

Its nest is a large stick platform usually in a tall tree. Normally two eggs are laid and these are, as so often with this family, greenish-blue. The single nestling I saw adopted a bittern-like posture as its parent sounded the alarm at my approach.

This large heron is holding its own and is quite common in northern Australia.

A single young in a large stick nest holds its head in a 'bitterning posture'.

11
GOLIATH HERON

Ardea goliath

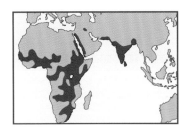

This big bird does very well in Africa, but in the Indian subcontinent it presents something of a mystery as nobody has found a nest, despite birds being seen quite often until recently. Only on a few large African lakes with convenient islands are more than one or two of these colorful birds seen together.

Identification

Length: minimum 140 cm (55 in)

The largest of living herons is by far the most colorful of the larger herons. The head is dark chestnut colored with a bushy crest on the crown. The neck is paler above and white from the chin downwards with black streaks along the front of the neck. The white lanceolate feathers on the upper breast hang down on to the deep rufous brown belly. The back and wings are a steely gray.

The huge bill is black and the lores yellow, as are the eyes. The legs and feet are black. Immature birds are duller with less well-defined markings.

Distribution, status and habitat conservation

Patchily distributed south of the Sahara desert, this giant of a heron is certainly not uncommon. It also occurs along the Red Sea coastlines and many have even bred in Iraq; there have also been sightings in Israel. On the Indian subcontinent, where it has been reported continuously from Pakistan to Sri Lanka, its position whether as a visitor or a spasmodic breeder is quite unknown. No nests have ever been found there, and indeed there are no records of regular migration.

These huge birds do not stray away from water. They live near shallow rivers and lakes, both fresh and salt marshes, creeks, estuaries and water holes. Africans, except under unusual circumstances, do not deliberately interfere with bird life and this heron is not harassed to any extent.

Feeding

The Goliath Heron is a solitary feeder, needing a fairly large territory usually of more than a square mile (2.6 km²). Only at nesting times do they feed together. Very large fish are speared, although mammals, amphibians and birds are taken at times. Smaller prey, whether fish or mammals, are ignored.

Breeding

Their infrequent courtship display indicates that this species retains its pair bonding over a number of years. Aggressive displays such as Forward, Fluffed Neck and Upright Stances are used frequently .

It is usually a solitary nester but there are some loose colonies on bigger lakes although this is not common.

Large stick or reed-stem nests can be built in a wide variety of sites ranging from tall trees, bushes, reeds or quite often even on the ground. The ground sites are most usual on uninhabited islands away from ground predators.

Two to four pale blue eggs are laid. The young are fed infrequently by regurgitation into the nest.

Above:

This species is the largest of all herons.

Right:

An adult bird resting on Lake Naivasha in Kenya.

Left:
Very large fish are caught by this bird.

Below Left:
Gapping: no sound results from this bill opening.

Below Right:
A pair at their nest in the Kruger National Park, South Africa.

12
PURPLE HERON

Ardea purpurea

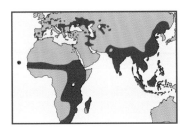

A surprisingly wide-ranging species, the Purple Heron is found throughout the Old World, although stopping short of Australia where other similar species take its place. It is a much shyer, retiring heron than its larger Old World neighbor, the Grey Heron. It often has its prey stolen by the larger bird if they are feeding close to each other and so it is inclined to skulk using its multicolored plumage as camouflage. On the other hand, it will vigorously defend its feeding territory from one of its own kind, puffing out its neck feathers and raising its crown aggressively.

Identification

Length: 79 cm (31 in)

The head and snake-like neck are the brightest feature of this medium to large heron. These are a strong orange-brown with a black cap and two prominent black stripes, one from the eye across the back of the neck and the other from the white chin down to the breast. The upper neck is speckled black-and-white and merges into the chestnut and white breast feathers. The lower breast and flanks are dark chestnut and the belly and under-tail black. The flight feathers are very dark gray and the under-wing coverts are mostly chestnut. The bill is yellow with a horn-brown culmen and tip. The eye is yellow, the lores green and the legs and feet dark brown. These colors all brighten during courtship and breeding. The toes are especially long.

Juvenile plumage is mainly brown and lacks the black head cap and neck stripes.

The oriental race *manilensis* has the neck stripes broken or absent, and is much paler. The Madagascan race *madagascariensis* is altogether darker in color, thus the striping is less obvious.

Distribution, status and habitat conservation

The Purple Heron breeds patchily in Europe, Asia and Africa. Much less common than formerly, its long and hazardous migrations between Africa and Europe have subjected it to severe drought conditions in Africa. In Asia, its long migration routes, such as the one from southern China to the far north-east to the Zhalong reserve, is extremely dangerous across hostile territory. Here, its young hatch in late July and must quickly depart southwards to avoid the rapidly arriving icy conditions.

Feeding

This heron prefers shallow, usually fresh water, with plenty of tall cover during the breeding season, but feeds more openly at other times. Such habitats are under constant threat from drainage and pollution, and numbers have fallen accordingly. Its very varied diet consists of fish, small rodents and reptiles as well as insects. Its bill is strong enough to tackle crustaceans and to kill quite large snakes. Its white speckled neck is fluffed up, not only when defending its feeding territory but also as part of its courtship display.

Breeding

This heron will nest singly but the species is found more commonly in colonies and prefers dense reedbeds and other thick vegetation, especially in parts of Asia and Africa. However, it does nest in trees. The nest is constructed of twigs, and the eggs number from two to five and are pale blue-green.

Above:
Adult bird.

Above Right:
In flight.

Right:
Some Purple Herons
nest in trees but
more often in reed
beds.

Left:

Young in a reed nest
in a colony in
northern China.

Below:

Feeding in
marshland in
Bharatpur, India.

Feeding territorial dispute. The neck is fluffed up aggressively.

13
GREAT WHITE EGRET

Egretta alba

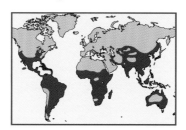

Is it a heron or is it an egret? Its behavior in Europe and Asia suggests that it is the largest of the egrets and its elegant displays seem to confirm this. In the New World however, it appears to take on the role of a more sedate heron. All over the world the plume-hunters have slaughtered it, so that even today numbers remain much smaller than in earlier times.

Identification

Length: 85–102 cm (33–40 in)

This large egret is all white and has spectacular plumes when breeding. The color of its legs and feet, as well as its bill, vary considerably both geographically, where well-defined races exist, and according to the season when breeding and courtship colors alter. These differences easily separate the different races in the field if care is taken in observation. Of the four well-defined races the New World race *egretta* is the largest. It has all black legs, a yellow bill that turns reddish pink when breeding and the lores become bright green.

The African race *melanorhynchos* also has all black legs but the bill turns black as breeding commences.

The European and temperate Asian bird *alba* has its legs variably colored. The tarsus is dark brown turning to black, while the tibia changes from dull yellow to vivid red during courtship. The yellow bill changes to pink with a black tip.

The small race *modesta* has a yellow bill which becomes black when breeding and its dusky legs turn black and then bright red.

The plumes are very long on the back and breast but there are no head plumes differentiating it from the Great Blue Heron, which does have a head crest when breeding in its all-white phases

Distribution, status and habitat conservation

The four races are spread around the world. In North America it nests south of Oregon, Minnesota and Maine through the rest of the country and then on into Central America, the Caribbean and throughout most of South America. In Europe it nests in Austria and Italy, and eastward into Russia. It is not common anywhere here, although its presence in northern Italy is encouraging. It is found in the Gulf States and in most of Africa south of the Sahara. The eastern race is spread right across the Indian subcontinent, all of South-East Asia and Australasia as far as the south island of New Zealand. It is a bird of the wetlands, although not averse to moving on to dryer land to feed. Nearly everywhere it is patchy in its distribution. Whether the birds in the New World have a different behavior from those in the rest of the World, and most particularly the smaller eastern race, is open to debate and much more study is required.

Feeding

This egret has all the techniques needed to catch its diverse prey. It takes mostly fish, but reptiles, small mammals, water and dry land insects and small birds are also taken. To do this, it will Walk Slowly or Quickly, Hop, Jump, Foot Stir, Wing Flick, Foot Paddle, Head Tilt and Peer Over. It will even hover, dip or plunge.

Breeding

The courtship displays are equally diverse and include Upright, Arched Neck and Forward displays. These and many others are extremely spectacular and include the erection of display plumes with raised wings. It is puzzling that only the eastern race appears to perform the Aerial Stretch display.

The stick nest is usually lined with grasses placed either in a tree, a bush or hidden in reeds.

Two to five pale blue eggs are laid. The nestlings are covered in white down and have a yellow bill. Their habit of climbing out of the nest results in a high mortality as they fall into the water to be eaten by waiting reptiles or onto land where a host of predators await.

The Eastern race
modesta with young
at Bharatpur, India.
The upper leg is
pale.

Right:

A male in full courtship plumage in Florida.

Below:

A courting pair of the race *egretta* in the USA. The bill above is black, as are the legs.

Left:
The Eastern race *modesta* in courtship colours with a black bill, bright green lores and pink legs. It is now much rarer in Japan.

Below Left:
A nonbreeding great White Egret with an immature Pied Egret in Australia.

Below Right:
Egret capturing a large fish.

Right:
Egret with a Florida scrub lizard.

Below Left:
Newly hatched young and egg.

Below Right:
Three young nestlings.

14
REDDISH EGRET

Egretta rufescens

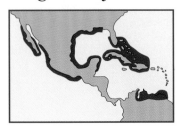

In the breeding season, which can be a long one, you can see greeting ceremonies where these birds toss and shake their heads at one another. They circle round with their beautiful crests erect. Along the coastline of the Southern States and part of Central and South America the numbers of this charming egret are still very small.

Identification

Length: 69–81 cm (27–32 in)

For some reason many species of coastal egrets are dimorphic. In the Reddish Egret the white phase is all white; the bill is black, the legs very dark and the lores are yellow. When the long head, neck and black plumes grow in time for breeding, the bill turns flesh color but the tip remains black. The legs are dark blue. The dark phase is somewhat variable. The head and neck vary from light tawny color to a deep reddish brown, the body and wings from slaty to bluish gray. The bill is dark or flesh colored with the tip black and the legs dark. These birds take 3 years to mature fully and the colors brighten with age. In breeding plumage, all the plumes become shaggy and lengthen and brighten. The bill turns pink with a black tip, the lores are a startling violet color and the legs turn cobalt blue, with the feet black on top and blue beneath.

Distribution, status and habitat conservation

Now happily extending its range, the Reddish Egret nests in Southern Florida south of Merritt Island and on the islands in Tampa Bay. It also occurs along the Gulf of Mexico from Texas through Mexico and Belize, with some birds breeding in Honduras and Panama. On the Pacific coast it breeds in Baja California south to El Salvador. It is found also in the Bahamas and Greater Antilles, and along the northern coast of Venezuela and Columbia. Many birds move south for winter, migrating back to their breeding grounds early in the year. They prefer open barren shallow flats along the coast which are wind-tidal and very salty. The mid-day temperature of these waters, which are no more than 15 cm (6 in) deep, can reach well over 38°C (100°F).

Feeding

Small fish are the main diet and these are usually captured in energetic style with Running, Hopping, Open-wing Feeding, and when Walking Slowly Foot Raking.

Breeding

A twig nest is built in long shrubs on islands. Two to six greenish-blue eggs are laid. This is preceded by many diverse courtship displays which include Circle Flights and Pursuit Flights at high speed, zigzagging as they go.

Dark-phased bird in breeding plumage.

Left:
Nonbreeding white-phased bird feeding.

Below:
Dark bird sitting on eggs.

Right:
A clutch of three eggs.

Below Left:
Nonbreeding dark-phased bird.

Below Right:
Breeding birds gathering in the evening light.

15

PIED HERON

Egretta picata

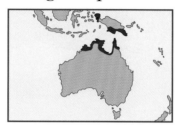

This is a 'top-end' bird of the Australian north although, like all Australians, it can be found casually almost anywhere north or south of its breeding areas.

Identification

Length: 48 cm (19 in)

The Pied Heron is an elegant black-and-white bird with bright yellow eyes, bill and legs. The head and body are black and the neck is pure white. In the young bird the head is brown and the underparts are pale slaty-colored or even white. Later, the body darkens while the head and neck become all white.

Plumes from the nape on the lower neck and across the back develop as the bird reaches the courtship stages, while the iris turns orange-red. The bright sheen of the slaty-blue plumes is particularly noticeable.

Distribution, status and habitat conservation

It would appear that the main breeding grounds of this species are along the tropical coastline of northern Australia where it appears to have an extended nesting period. Its northern migration takes it to southern Borneo, the Celebes and New Guinea but nesting is unlikely here. A few birds wander further north or southwards into the Australian hinterland.

It prefers shallow water whether fresh or salt. It will feed on flooded grasslands but its favorite habitats are sewage farms, animal stockyards and garbage tips.

Feeding

Small fish and frogs but mainly insects, are taken by Walking Quickly or Slowly, Foot Stirring or Peering Over. At sewage farms they were observed 'capturing' what appeared to be offal by hovering above the water.

When feeding with other egrets particularly Little Egrets, they are frequently chased away only to return immediately to steal again. As successful feeders they regularly roost between meals when their aggression subsides.

Breeding

Two to four dark blue-green eggs are laid in a neat, well-lined nest of twigs. The nest is usually sited near or very often above water in mangroves or other bushes. Breeding occurs in mixed colonies of egrets and cormorants, with kites and other predators and scavengers roosting around them. I found immature birds at all stages of growth in one colony, while some birds were still sitting on eggs and cooing gently.

Adult bird.

Left: At the nest in northern Australia.

Below: At the sewage farm in Darwin, Australia.

Above Right: Fighting with a Little
Egret.

Below: Adult and immature birds
with Little Egrets.

Left: Immature birds have all white heads.

Below: Young bird just fledged.

16
SLATY EGRET

Egretta vinaceigula

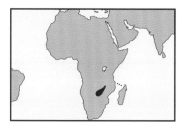

Only in recent years has this unobtrusive egret become known, and even then not very well. It lives in swamps south of the African lakes. Believe it or not, it was more or less ignored until less than 30 years ago.

Identification

Length: 43 cm (17 in)

Only recently recognized as a separate species, which is strange since the Slaty Egret does not resemble the Black Heron in the slightest. It is a pale blue-gray bird with a vinous chin, throat and fore-neck. Its eyes, legs and feet are yellow. The bill is black or dark gray.

Modest lanceolate plumes develop on nape, neck and back when breeding. It has shrill triple call when disturbed.

Distribution, status and habitat conservation

The Slaty Egret occupies swamps and flood plains in a small area of southern Africa; it is known to breed in the Okovango swamps, Botswana, and has been sighted northwards to the Chobe National Park, Namibia. It certainly visits the flood plains on the Zambezi River, Zambia and also southern Angola. Wanderers have been seen to the south and west of this somewhat restricted territory and it may well either migrate regularly or seek out flood areas after breeding. Much more study is needed to clarify its distribution.

Feeding

The Slaty Egret has generally been observed to feed in parties of four to six birds. It Walks Slowly to catch fish and appears to Foot Stir on a regular basis. Snails are gleaned from water-lily leaves and Standing Flycatching for dragonflies has been noted. Described as a "fidgety" hunter it runs about with wings partially open. As it often has time to perch regularly in trees, it is assumed to be an efficient feeder. What factors restrict it to such a small range are yet to be learned.

Breeding

Three nestlings were found in a nest in a thicket of wild figs in northern Botswana and a small colony was seen in a reedbed up the Chobe river from Kasane, Namibia. Such sparse knowledge leaves much work to be done.

Above: Showing
vinous colored
throat and yellow
legs.

Left: Feeding in
Botswana.

17
BLACK HERON

Egretta ardesiaca

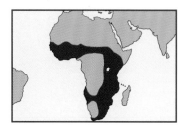

Several egrets open their wings when feeding but only this unique species forms a completely enclosed canopy when fishing. Its bill is then thrust vertically downwards to catch small fish. From time to time it will stop and shake itself like a dog.

Identification

Length: 48–50 cm (19–20 in)

The Black Heron has all-black plumage, legs, bill and lores. Its bright yellow iris and feet thus stand out sharply. The feet turn red when courtship commences. The lanceolate plumes on the crown and nape are quite luxuriant. The flight feathers, which enable this unique heron to form a complete canopy above its head when feeding, are broad veined.

Distribution, status and habitat conservation

The Black Heron ranges over much of South Africa south of the Sahara, but avoids forests and deserts. On some rivers and lakes it may remain all year round but more often its movements are sporadic. Quite why this occurs is not known. I have watched well-established territorial feeders along the shores of Lake Jipe, on the Kenyan side, while parties of exhausted birds recovered nearby, before departing the following day. Just as jet black African Open-billed Storks range across the continent searching for snails, so it appears many Black Herons follow similar patterns searching for shallow-water feeding areas. Along the coast near Durban, South Africa, as well as in west Africa, they fish in the sea.

Feeding

The wings go up and down, forming a complete canopy under which the shaded head is buried. The bill strikes downward to catch prey between its open mandibles. Very occasionally it feeds without this elaborate movement, usually when it eats crustaceans or aquatic insects. The frequent rearrangement of the feathers seems to necessitate regular shaking and preening.

Although usually a freshwater feeder, shoals of small fish along the coast attract it in some numbers to Durban, South Africa, where an exciting leap-frogging performance can be observed at the right time of year, and small flocks of migrating birds feed together along the West African coastline.

Breeding

Sadly, we lack knowledge of the courtship display which, given the dexterity of its wings, could be of much interest.

In mixed colonies, I have usually found that this bird tucks itself well back into the foliage of a tree. The nest is a solid one of twigs and can sometimes be in mangroves or bushes. Human disturbance of previously very large breeding colonies of Black Herons has resulted in smaller numbers mixing among other species.

The dark blue eggs are usually only three to a clutch.

Dark-plumed adult
at Lake Jipe, Kenya.

Left: Wing spread. Raised leg shows yellow foot.

Below Left: Peering over with wings spread.

Below: A full 'umbrella' stance with bill pointing vertically down.

Right: Fish grasped in bill.

Below: A group of feeding birds on the West African coast.

18
TRICOLORED HERON

Egretta tricolor

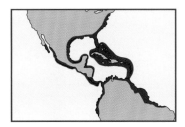

Although found mainly along coastlines, in fresh water and salt water this very demonstrative bird will wade deeply and sometimes even swim for its prey. It is not quite as active as the Reddish Egret, but it is a close second.

Previously called the Louisiana Heron, its quite wide range precludes this state from an exclusive claim to its name, although many think 'Tricolor' a poor substitute.

Identification

Length: 60–70cm (24–28 in)

Slaty gray on its head, neck, wings, back and tail, the Tricolored Heron has a white belly, rump and under-wing. Down the front of the neck is a white and rufous-colored line and this same rufous color develops on the lower neck covering the chest extending onto the wings. The plumes on the mane, back and lower neck thicken to form a brighter rufous color during breeding.

The yellow bill with its brown tip then turns bright blue with matching lores, but the tip becomes black. The full red eye brightens markedly and the yellow legs turn bright red. (It really does put on a show during courtship).

Distribution, status and habitat conservation

Very much a coastal species, the range of the race *ruficollis* stretches along the Atlantic coast of North America from Florida north to Maine. It is found all around the Gulf of Mexico states and westwards north to Baja California, and throughout the Caribbean. The nominate race is found in most of Central America and around the coasts of South America, southwards in the west as far as Peru and in the east to northern Brazil.

Of the two races, *ruficollis* from the north migrates southward in the winter. It prefers shallow marshes, mudflats and tidal creeks. While by no means a rare bird, it is outnumbered by the Little Blue Heron over most of its range.

Feeding

Although this heron prefers shallow water it will certainly venture into quite deep water. Furthermore it is not above taking advantage of grebes and other diving birds that disturb fish and send them within reach. When capturing fish it engages in the widest variety of feeding techniques of all the egrets. It eats amphibians, reptiles, crustaceans and insects rather more sedately.

Breeding

Courtship displays involve Upright and Forward Aggression. Snap and Stretch displays are somewhat unusually merged into one movement. Bill Clappering and Crest Raising complete a full repertoire.

A flat platform of twigs in trees or bushes is the usual place for this egret to lay its three to four greenish-blue eggs, although it will use very low foliage or even the ground if larger sites are not available and protection is provided.

When hatched, the chicks are easily distinguished by their white bellies and dark gray wings and body. Young birds begin clambering at 3–4 weeks old and often fall from the nest to be snapped up by waiting predators.

Above: A breeding bird shields its eggs.

Above Right: Grown nestlings begging for food.

Right: An immature bird just fledged.

Left Page

Above Right: A breeding bird. The bill turns blue with a black tip

Above Left: Commensal feeding with Florida Moorhen.

Left: An adult bird catching small fish.

19
INTERMEDIATE EGRET

Egretta intermedia

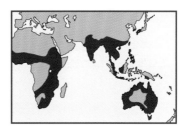

This Old World white egret causes immense confusion to the birdwatchers of the Old World. It has three easily distinguished races mainly separated only by bill and leg color. Here lies the trouble, for its African name of Yellow-billed Egret will not suffice in Eurasia where the bill turns completely black during the breeding season, and its Australian name of Plumed Egret holds good only during the breeding season. To tell the races apart and to distinguish this often widespread bird from the larger Great White Egret is quite a feat.

Identification

Length: 65–72 cm (26–28 in)

The Eurasian race, like the other two, is all white. The legs are all black and the yellow bill turns gradually black as the breeding season approaches. The long breeding plumes are more on the back and the neck, but not on the head. The lores turn from yellow to green in all three races.

The African race changes the color of its legs from brown to yellow and then red as breeding approaches. The bill is then a fiery red.

The Australian race is almost exactly the same as the African race and could well be the same race. To distinguish it from the Great White Egret at all times check the skin around the eye. In the Intermediate Egret it stops at the eye but in the Great White Egret it forms a prominent line, extending to well behind the eye.

The Australians called their bird the Plumed Egret because its plumes are thicker and larger than the Great White Egret, but this is only a temporary phase in breeding plumage.

Distribution, status and habitat conservation

The Intermediate Egret breeds patchily in Africa south of the Sahara avoiding jungle and desert where the race is a distinctive one (*brachyryncha*).

The nominate race, *intermedia,* ranges across all of the Indian subcontinent and through most of South-East Asia, northwards to Japan and down to the Philippines. The most attractive race, particularly when breeding, is the Australian *plumifera* which occupies all of Australia, except the dry center, as well as islands to the north below Wallace's Line to New Guinea, although it does not breed there.

Northern birds migrate to the north to join the Asian race coming south from Japan. A bird of the wetlands, whether fresh or salt, it ranges through all such habitats. I have found it outnumbers the Great White Egret in most habitats, although in Japan it appears to be more threatened than its larger relation.

Feeding

Although it is normally a sedate bird which Walks Slowly, it sometimes has a distinctive strut like the Black-headed Heron. This quite elegant movement appears designed to display its distinctive neck plumes to full advantage.

It eats mainly fish but frogs, water insects and grasshoppers are also taken, particularly as food for the nestlings.

Breeding

These birds invariably nest in mixed colonies with other herons and egrets. Considerable aggressive behavior occurs during pair bonding and their plume fanning is a particularly spectacular feature. Buzzing calls are given during a wide variety of displays including Upright, Forward, Flap Flight, Twig Shaking, Snap, Stretch and Circle Flights. Mutual preening, neck intertwining and Bill Clappering round off this extensive range of behavior.

The nest is made of twigs or reeds according to location. It can be placed in reeds, low vegetation or quite tall trees, often over waterlogged ground. Two to four pale sea-green eggs are laid.

Breeding plumed 'Yellow Billed' Egret in Africa.

Right:
'Plumed Egret' in Australia with yellow lores in breeding dress.

BelowLeft:
African race with pale tarsus and all yellow bill. The lores are green.

Below Right:
Nonbreeding bird of the nominate race in Indonesia.

Left: Nonbreeding bird in India. The legs are all black.

Below: A bird in courtship plumes with bill nearly black. The legs are also black in this nominate race which stretches from South-East Asia to Northern India.

Above: The Intermediate Egret is the commonest egret at this colony in Bharatpur, India.

Left: A breeding bird with young at the nest in India. The black color is fading towards the tip.

20

WHITE-FACED HERON

Egretta novaehollandiae

This most widespread of Australian herons can usually be found along the coast in winter, but it comes inland to breed. Its occupation of New Zealand began in the early 1940s and now it is found everywhere there provided that there are trees. Most of its behavior is little known, perhaps because of its unobtrusive nature.

Identification

Length: *c.* 66 cm (26 in)

Slender and more graceful than the larger members of its family, the White-faced Heron is a blue-gray bird with white on the front of the head, chin and round the eye; underparts are pale gray. There is a small patch of light chestnut feathering at the base of the neck which flows over the upper breast. Short gray lanceolate plumes on the back do not reach the tail.

In flight, the black tips to the flight feathers, their white centers and gray fore-edge give a barred effect. Immature birds lack the bronze and gray plumes, and the pale gray belly has a brownish tinge.

The black bill sometimes has a yellow tip. During breeding yellow eye and yellow feet and legs brighten and become reddish for a time, although the plumes do not lengthen.

The two races described are frankly hard to separate.

Low-pitched calls are issued with a high-pitched alarm call uttered on the wing.

Distribution, status and habitat conservation

Common and widespread throughout Australia, Tasmania and New Zealand, this bird is also well established in Papua New Guinea. The breeding colony on New Caledonia has given rise to a suggested separate subspecies but this is of doubtful validity. It disperses quite widely but no pattern of migration has been established. It uses coastal mudflats on which to feed, but moves inland to freshwater habitats to breed.

Feeding

This species forages by Standing, Walking Slowly, either Upright or Crouched. It will sometimes Walk Quickly or Run. It Foot Stirs, Head Tilts and Wing Flicks. It defends well-spaced territories, although abundant prey will attract it in some numbers.

Shrimps, crabs, insects, spiders and snails are eaten. In particular, the tree frog, introduced from Australia to New Zealand, has probably played a large part in its expansion there. Despite all this, fish is still the major food source and these include trout.

Breeding

While there are no notable displays, Twig Offering and Courtship Flight precedes nesting, which is spread over as much as an 8-month period. White-faced Herons nest singly; or in groups; the nest is a platform of twigs in a tall tree. From two to six blue to greeny-white eggs are laid.

Above Right: Feeding in northern Australia.

Above Left: This species wanders north after the rains.

Left: An adult White-faced Heron in southern Australia.

21
LITTLE BLUE HERON

Egretta caerulea

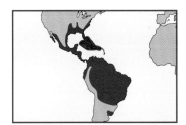

The Little Blue Heron is a bit of an individualist, not always conforming to the behavior established by other similar species. I sat on a boat in the Corina Swamp, Trinidad, and watched the Scarlet Ibis come into roost. Immediately afterwards other species arrived, including herons, and the contrast in arrival patterns was most marked. As Snowy Egrets came along they formed a tight determined group like a squadron of fighter planes, but the Little Blues came in ones and twos zigzagging between the mangrove islands, climbing and diving before making up their minds where they were to settle.

Identification

Length: 64–71 cm (25–29 in)

The Little Blue Heron is certainly not all blue, except from a distance. Seen close-up, the head and neck are reddish brown once the bird has reached full maturity as a 2 year old. Legs and feet are gray green, the lores are dull green and the eye yellow. The light gray bill has a distinctive black tip and this quickly identifies it both in its mature reddish brown and blue plumage, and in its first year when it is all white. After this the plumage becomes speckled with individual blue feathers before a final molt into its mature state.

Distribution, status and habitat conservation

In North America, breeding occurs in the eastern coastlands of the Gulf of California, the shore of the Gulf of Mexico, the southern Mississippi basin, all of Florida and northwards along the Atlantic coast as far as Massachusetts. In recent years it has expanded its range inland from the Atlantic coast. Its range extends all the way south through central and South America, as far as Lima, Peru, in the west and Uruguay in the East. Some birds have been seen as far south as Argentina, possibly in concert with the Cattle Egret's expansion. It is very abundant in the West Indies and migrants from the north join breeding birds in the winter.

Feeding

Along the open mudflats of Sanibel Island at low tide you can see a polka-dot pattern of blue-and-white birds as these herons feed interspersed with White Ibis. They feed on the full range of fish, amphibians and insects and vary their techniques accordingly. On the island of Tobago, for example, they move individually quite slowly along the edges of the freshwater streams but when the fishermen haul in their nets in the evening, they sit on the boats moored in the bay ready to land near the nets as small wriggling fish escape onto the sand.

Breeding

Their breeding behavior mirrors their general habits. In the colonies much intermarital copulation occurs in this promiscuous species, which perhaps typifies its somewhat nonconformist behavior. Nests are built in a wide variety of sites and are usually of twigs. They are quite flimsy platforms and into them are laid two to five pale blue eggs.

Right: The evening light reflects from the sea, lightening the blue of the back.

Below: Along the sea-coast in Tobago. The bill is turning blue and the tip markedly black.

Above: Feeding by 'peering' over.

Left: This unusual breeding bird with blue bill, has a white neck and head replacing the normal reddish plumage.

Above: A Little Blue Heron catching crayfish that live below the 'lettuce' plants in the Corkscrew Swamp.

Right: For the first year, this species is all white. The black tip to the bill and the very pale legs separate it from other white egrets.

103

22
SNOWY EGRET

Egretta thula

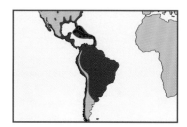

This delightful high-stepping bird is the busiest feeder of America's white herons. An attractive bird when dressed in its smart breeding plumage, it gives a most harsh 'aah' cry and it displays its finery aggressively at the slightest excuse.

Identification

Length: 56–66 cm (22–26 in)

The Snowy Egret is a medium-sized, all-white bird with a black bill and legs, and yellow feet – the yellow often extending well up the back of the leg. Its lores are dull yellow, brightening as the breeding season approaches, and then frequently flushing orange or red, as do its feet. At that time it grows thick head plumes and re-curved back and neck plumes.

The race *brewsteri* from lower California is somewhat larger.

Distribution, status and habitat conservation

Widespread and numerous in North America, the Snowy Egret occurs as a breeding bird from Maine to Florida, from Texas to the Gulf of Mexico, along the California coast and well inland to several western states.

Southwards in Central America, the Caribbean and in South America it is much less common and more patchily distributed although some birds do breed as far south as Argentina.

This bird was badly affected by the plume hunters, but owing to active conservation has recovered and indeed increased in numbers within the United States. However, further south the plume trade continued for many years and this undoubtedly delayed its return to abundance in the West Indies and South America. Pollution in these areas may also have played its part; in Idaho, USA, some returning migrants may have failed to breed for just this reason.

Feeding

The most active of feeders, surpassed only by the Reddish Egret, the Snowy Egret has a wide range of feeding behavior. It uses its yellow feet extensively to disturb prey by Stirring, Raking, Probing and Paddling. It will perform foot movements while hovering on the wing. It even vibrates its bill in the water to attract fish.

Its diet is diverse. Small fish, crabs, molluscs, aquatic insects and frogs, as well as crayfish and snakes, are supplemented by terrestrial insects caught when following cattle or other animals.

Breeding

As breeding begins this egret performs spectacular aerial displays. It nests in close proximity to other birds in the colony, resulting in fierce and aggressive fights. The stick nest is built comparatively low down in trees or bushes, and three to five blue-green eggs are laid.

This bird has partly flushed lores and feet. The yellow turning orange before becoming a deep red. Thick plumes on the neck distinguish it from other white egrets.

Left: Often called 'the bird with the yellow slippers'.

Right: An aggressive bird with crest raised and fiery red lores.

Below: A well-plumed bird with yellow lores.

Right: Regular aeriel fights occur between Snowy Egrets.

Below: Young nestlings have yellow bills. The elder chick's bill has already turned black and the younger one's bill will do so in a day or so.

23
LITTLE EGRET

Egretta garzetta

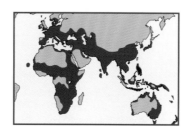

There is a real upheaval underway in the complex world of the Little Egret. Coastal habitat destruction is forcing its 'reef heron' forms to move back to land-based colonies and a rare mixture of color and shape is being created. The ornithological establishment is currently turning many a blind eye to the situation, presumably waiting for a plausible explanation to be put forward for this phenomenon and its taxonomic implications.

Identification

Length: 55–65 cm (22–26 in)

The trouble started back in 1833, when Edward Lear painted a Little Egret for John Gould's *Birds of Europe*. Unfortunately, Lear copied a skin sent from Australia, thus starting the confusion between races which has bedevilled authors and artists alike ever since, and which still results in some major errors in both published texts and paintings.

There are three quite distinct all-white races of this widely distributed species.

1) — The nominate race *garzetta garzetta*: This race is all white. Its bill is completely black, as are its legs, while its eyes and feet are yellow. It has blue-gray lores. In breeding dress the lores turn pink or often bright red; when this color fades, the skin is pale or colorless and sometimes and, in some lights, it reflects the sun and *appears* to have color. At this time, the feet, which similarly turn pink or red, also fade back to dull yellow. The plumes developed on the throat, back and nape recede at different intervals, very often depending on the age of the individual bird.

First-year birds have a greenish-colored bill with black markings, and the lores can be pale green before darkening. The legs are similarly dull black and green.

2) — The Indonesian race *garzetta nigripes*: This race is identical to the nominate race expect that its feet are black. The occasional individual has yellow soles.

3) — The Australian race *garzetta immaculata*: This race, the one depicted by Edward Lear, has bright yellow lores and black feet; again, the soles are sometimes yellow. Its plumes during breeding are usually somewhat more spectacularly developed than those of the nominate race, hence its name *immaculata* (meaning, literally, spotless and therefore intimating true beauty.)

In addition to these all-white races, there are three further races which are dimorphic. Each has an all-white phase and a dark blue phase, and often a mixed phase as well. These are basically coastal birds and are called reef herons.

4) — The island race *garzetta dimorpha*: All-white birds of this race occasionally have a few odd dark feathers. The dark birds are dark blue with a white throat patch; some individuals have a white wing patch on the carpal joint on one or both wings. Intermediate birds are paler, and their plumage is a mix of blue and white.

All these phases have a jet-black bill and legs, with yellow feet and the lores are yellow. They grow breeding plumes in similar fashion to the all-white races.

The nestlings of this race are quite distinctive. All have quite large legs and feet, which are usually green but can be black. Their plumage can vary from all white to all dark blue and to a highly speckled dark and white feathering. This plumage is molted after the first year either to all white or to all blue, or to mixed plumage, although this last phase is rare.

5) — The West African race *garzetta gularis*: This is the classic Reef Heron. The dark phase, which predominates over most of its range, is almost identical to the race *dimorpha*, except for its bill and legs, which are never black but range in color from yellow to dark brown, turning even darker when breeding. The feet are, like the lores, a dull yellow. The rarer white phase often has a few dark feathers and is found more often in the north of its range.

6) — The Indian/Middle Eastern race *garzetta schistacea*: This race is almost impossible to typify and has never been properly assessed. The conclusion is that its widely varying colors are a result of its interbreeding in a number of areas with the nominate race seems now to be beyond doubt, but this is fiercely disputed in some quarters and somewhat indifferently in others. It certainly has the most varied coloration of soft parts of any race, irrespective of whether the plumage is all white or dark blue.

Bill colour varies from black through to brown and from yellow to pale green. Some birds have a faintly marked dark tip to the bill, while others have a quite distinctive dark tip extending up to one-third of the length of the bill. This pattern is seen in Little Blue Herons and Reddish Egrets as well as Swinhoe's Egret, but in the case of the last two it fades after breeding is completed. Whether this is so with *schistacea* Little Egrets, or is found in some juvenile birds and then fades, has not been established and needs investigation, Bill thickness, particularly at the base of the bill, is also a variable feature, while some individuals have a slightly decurved upper mandible.

Leg color is equally diverse and certainly does not correlate with bill color. Most *schistacea* have faint or bright yellow feet, but not all. Yellow feet turn red or pink during courtship.

Most adult birds have yellow lores, but on others they can be blue-gray or colorless. In all cases the lores turn red during the courtship period but fade as eggs are laid.

Young dark-plumaged birds have pale breast and underparts at least in the first year, and do not grow courtship plumes at this time. Nevertheless, this does not prevent the lores from reddening, nor does it inhibit the execution of mating ceremonies, such as stick exchanges.

Distribution, status and habitat conservation

The nominate all-white race is in the process of expanding its range. In Europe it now breeds in northern France and has spread from here to Britain and Ireland, where small colonies have become established in the last few years. Some birds have been seen in North America and the Caribbean, and there are reports of it breeding in Barbados and Jamaica. Contrary to some statements, the nominate Little Egret can be found in both freshwater and saltwater habitats.

Most of the other races are mainly sedentary except for the race *schistacea*, which has adapted to mainland breeding in western India following the destruction of its natural habitat of coastal mangroves. Birds of this race have been recorded in Africa as far south as the Kenyan lakes. However, the few dark birds found in America and the Caribbean could be of the West African race *gularis* and since it was from there that the spectacular movement of the Cattle Egrets to the New World originated some years ago, this seems more than likely .

Broadly, the races are distributed as follows, The nominate race is found in warm and temperate climates all over Europe, southern Asia and Africa. The race *nigripes* centres around Indonesia northwards to the Philippines, and the race *immaculata* is restricted to Australia and New Zealand. The race *dimorpha* inhabits many of the islands off the coast of East Africa and the race *gularis* occupies the coastline of much of West Africa, but the race *schistacea* is found throughout the Middle East, East Africa, the west coast of India and parts of the Indian east coast as far as Calcutta.

The situation is not, however that straightforward. In Israel, dark birds have appeared from the south and particoloured individuals have been recorded. Detailed investigation into where and how racial integration takes place and what forms result has yet to be undertaken in a serious manner. Certainly, a particoloured bird in Israel had many characteristics of a nominate Little Egret and this may be due to the intrusion of individual dark birds into an all-white colony, with the resultant offspring having predominantly nominate *garzetta* genes. On the other hand, in western India, the intrusion of a small number of all-white nominate race birds into a *schistacea*-dominated colony may have produced some egrets with predominantly *schistacea* genes, as well as others with a preponderance of nominate *garzetta* genes.

None of this can be proved beyond doubt until intensive work on the DNA of these egrets is undertaken. Meanwhile, the extensive field work carried out by the late Professor Naik and his students in western India has gone very largely unnoticed internationally. In the summer of 1998, however, a bird arrived in southern England which brought the situation into more prominence. This all-white egret had greenish-yellow lores, a bright yellow bill with a prominent dark tip, and legs and feet which were light green. It was initially considered to be a 'Western Reef Heron' by the very many birdwatchers who observed it closely, using high-powered telescopes. It may be marginally larger than its nominate Little Egret companions seen feeding nearby, but it most certainly presents itself as a nominate *garzetta* form and not the somewhat heavier *schistacea* form. It is without doubt different in appearance from any other 'Western Reef Heron' that I have seen among the many hundreds that I have looked at either in the wild or as museum skins, but its greenish-yellow lores, not found on either adult or juvenile nominate birds, confirmed that it was a racially, mixed bird. Other forms may well appear as the species continues to expand its range.

Feeding

As would be expected with such a plastic species, the Little Egret has a wide variety of feeding techniques ranging from Standing and Waiting to quite rapid Running, sometimes with partly opened wings. It commonly uses Foot Stirring while standing in shallow water.

It eats small fish, insects, small mammals and small birds, and cracks open crustaceans with its large bill. While feeding communally Little Egrets will adopt an aggressive approach and when in breeding plumage use this to good effect in agonistic display.

Breeding

Little Egrets breed in many different habitat types. The stick nest can be on the ground, on rocks or on walls, but most often is placed in bushes or trees. Up to five greenish-blue eggs are laid. Chicks of coastal races develop a wide range of plumages according to their parentage, but most acquire either mainly dark blue or all-white plumes after their second moult.

———

It is my view that intensive research into this species could be extremely rewarding and that the Little Egret presents one of the greatest challenges to modern ornithologists.

Above:
Nominate race
garzetta with
nestlings.

Above Right:
Nominate race
nesting on rocks on
Lake Turkana,
East Africa.

Right:
Nominate race with
blue lores and
yellow feet.

Above Left:
Eggs of Little Egret,
in twig nest.

Above:
Feeding on fish left
after a fish-pond has
been drained in
Israel.

Left:
Australian race
immaculata catches
a fish.

Above Right:
Indonesia race *nigripes* show black feet.

Above Left:
Australian race *immaculata* in partial breeding plumes but with yellow lores and no head crest.

Right:
Immature *immaculata*. Bill turning black but still yellow at base. Legs still green. The legs of all young Little Egrets do this.

Above Left:
Mixed race bird in Israel.

Above:
Same bird in flight showing blue and white.

Left:
Race *schistacea*, in breeding colors: Red lores, yellow bill, black legs, red feet; no head plumes.

Above:
Dark and White Morphs, both with yellow bills in India.

Above Right:
White morphed *schistacea* with black bill and legs. Red legs and feet in courtship colours.

Right:
White morph displaying at dark morph. The bill of the white morph is pale, whereas the bill of the dark morph is yellow/red.

Left:
Pair of white morphs courting. Both have yellow/red bills.

Below Left:
White morph bird using plumes in aggressive display to defend chicks in nest Courtship colors of dark morph show this bird is not paired with this female.

Below:
White morph *schistacea* with yellow bill and red lores.

Above:
Nest colony of
mainly *schistacea*
birds in India.

Above Right:
Dark morph on a
nest built on
telephone pole due
to lack of nest space
in tree in India.

Right:
Dark morph
schistacea in
courtship garb.

Left:
Dark morph feeding chick out of nest.

Below Left:
Dark morph with dark chicks.

Below:
Dark and White morphs of *schistacea*.

Above:
Mixed morph
schistacea in
courtship colors.

Above Right:
Pair of dark morphs.
The red lores on bird
shielding eggs have
faded.

Right:
Twig passing
between adult dark
morph and
immature bird.

Above Left:
Race *dimorpha* on reef. Dark morph on Kisite Island, East Africa.

Above:
Dimorpha, white morph on Kisite Island, East Africa.

Left:
Young *schistacea* chick.

Above:
Group of dimorphic
birds on reef on
Kisite Island, East
Africa.

Right:
Mixed morph
dimorpha on Kisite
Island, East Africa.

Above:
Dark and White
morph chicks away
from nest at Kisite
Island, East Africa.

Left:
Two nestlings in nest
built in low island
vegetation on Kisite
Island, East Africa.

**All are of the race
dimorpha.**

Right:
Mixed morph bird flying at Kisite Island, East Africa.

Below:
White phase *dimorpha* with dark specs on Kisite Island, East Afica.

Above :
Race *gularis* feeding
in West Africa.

Above Right:
Dark race *Schistacea*
at Lake Turkana,
East Africa.

Right:
Dark morph
Schistacea with
white *garzetta* at
rock nest site at Lake
Turkana, East Africa.

Dark race *Schistacea* flying. This bird was once described as the elusive dark morph of *garzetta, garzetta*. It certainly breeds with the white birds on Lake Turkana. Specimens collected are in the Maimi Research Collections and are identified as *Schistacea*

This is the mixed race between the nominate race and *garzetta schistacea*. It was seen in Southern England in the summer of 1998. Its yellow lores clearly demonstrate its mixed origin.

127

24

SWINHOE'S OR CHINESE EGRET

Egretta eulophotes

In winter, a few of these birds feed on the mudflats alongside the airport in Singapore. It is a lively, almost hyperactive feeder, somewhat like the Reddish Egret, and it seems to catch its prey efficiently. It is hard to see why this quite ordinary white egret should have been so badly depleted in numbers compared with other similarly adorned members of its family. One might surmise that as a victim of the plume trade it was more ruthlessly exterminated over much of its range than many other egrets. In a part of the world where such savagery is seldom condemned, it may appear the likely explanation. An additional disadvantage of its elegant breeding plumage was that it encouraged local women to eat its eggs in the belief that they would enhance their looks. The eastern habit of eating parts of birds or animals in the mistaken idea that their strength, beauty or reproductive powers could be absorbed appears to be more widespread now that the influence of Buddhism has waned.

Identification

Length: 68 cm (27 in)

This is an all-white egret. The basal half of the lower mandible is flesh-colored or even yellow and the rest of the bill is black. The lores and legs are yellowish green and the eyes are also yellow. As breeding time approaches, the bill becomes bright yellow and the lores bright blue. The feet are yellow and the legs become blacken. The long, thick plumes from the nape are matched by similar neck and back plumes. The Eastern Reef Heron in its white phase has shorter, stubby greenish legs and is altogether a less elegant bird.

Distribution, status and habitat conservation

Swinhoe's Egret breeds only in a small area of South-East Asia where its true range is unknown. It has been completely exterminated over nearly the whole of its former range in China and, while a few birds have retreated to North Korea, its present numbers are pitifully small.

It migrates south after breeding and its winter stronghold appears to be in the mangroves in Bohol Province, the Philippines. Perhaps 1000 birds still exist and it is listed as an endangered species.

Feeding

A feeder mainly in very shallow tidal estuaries, mudflats and bays. It eats small fish which it chases with half-open wings. It also eats shrimps and crabs, but somewhat more sedately. It probably used rice fields in China at one time, but alas no more.

Breeding

It nests in tall trees, building a stick nest; though one of dry grass was reported from Korea. Three to five pale blue-green eggs are laid, but little else has been reported about this rare egret.

Left:
In breeding plumage. The well-plumed head feathers separate it from the Little Egret.

Below:
A nonbreeding bird in flight, in northern China.

25
EASTERN REEF HERON

Egretta sacra

This short-legged egret is found around coastlines, well spread out along reefs and rocky outcrops. In mangrove swamps, however, which have an abundance of food on the mudflats, numbers of them feed together. Whether dark or white morphs have different food preferences is doubtful. They will venture some way inland to visit rice fields, though along the Chinese coast this is a dangerous thing to do.

Identification

Length: 58 cm (23 in)

This is a very different looking bird from the so-called Western Reef Heron (*Egretta garzetta schistacea*). Although it is similarly dimorphic, it is a much shorter-legged bird and quite unlike the slender Little Egret family. The dark morph is slaty to brownish black with a thin white streak on its chin. I have found birds in Indonesia to be very much lighter than those in Australia.

The white morph is all white. The iris is yellow and the stubby legs more green than yellow. The soles of the feet are a brighter yellow. The bill varies in color from a dull yellow to a dark brown and the lores are a yellowish green.

During breeding, lanceolate and filamentous plumes develop on the lower fore-neck and back and a short tuft of plumes grows from the nape. In the dark morph the soft-parts brighten and in the white morphs the bill blackens.

Distribution, status and habitat conservation

A widespread coastal species, this reef heron ranges from the east coast of India throughout the rest of Asia and northwards through the Philippines to Japan. Southwards, its range extends around the coast of Australia and New Zealand. At the northern and southern extremities of its range the dark morph predominates; elsewhere an equal number of each phase are to be found.

This is basically a sedentary species which inhabits rocky coasts and coral reefs but also gathers on the tidal mudflats around mangroves, and is attracted to rice fields near to the coast.

Feeding

This species uses the usual wide range of techniques to capture its prey. It usually feeds alone, eating fish, crabs and most insects, but an abundance of food, including mudskippers, often attracts numbers of birds.

Both morphs feed together and in some areas I have seen the white morph concentrating on fish, although I do not think their food preferences differ according to their color. This leaves open the question of why white birds are found more often in tropical areas – another facet of the dimorphic conundrum that remains to be unraveled. With their short legs they prefer to stand on a rock and lean over when feeding but they are also prepared to wade in shallow water.

Breeding

Stick nests lined with grass or leaves are placed on almost any projection whether bush or small tree, rocky ledge or wooden pier. In Indonesia I found a nest at some height in the middle of a colony of a number of egret species.

The eggs are pale greenish blue and clutch sizes vary from two to as many as six. I found newly hatched chicks with dark gray down and flesh-colored bills and legs. The upper mandible was tipped black.

Above :
White phase bird
flying (northern
Australia).

Above Right:
Feeding is done
from a rock
whenever possible.

Right :
Peering over from
rock.

Above :
This bird is wading in shallow water. The legs are shorter than other egret species.

Left:
Dark phase bird flying.

Above:
Dark phase bird feeding from a rock needs wings out to retain balance.

Above Right:
White phase bird stalking along rocky coast in northern Australia.

Right:
This bird in mangroves in Indonesia is much paler than the Australian dark phase bird.

Left: The long neck and body contrast with the shorter legs on this dark phase bird.

Below: Like many estuarine feeders the bill tip on this species is black.

26
CATTLE EGRET

Bubulcus ibis

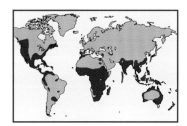

This little egret is one of life's winners. It spread into South America from Africa and then caused a big stir by invading North America where it was not universally welcomed. It expanded in the east in an equally spectacular manner. This aggressive bird captures most of its insect prey on dry land assisted by all sorts of animals, including man and his machines that stir things up nicely!

Identification

Length: 50 cm (20 in)

An all-white bird with a short yellow bill and black legs. Only when in breeding plumage can the two (or three) races be distinguished: the crown, back and chest turn buff-colored, and the bill and legs red. However, the eastern race which occurs in India eastward has a more pronounced, darker, deeper buff which is spread widely over the neck and chest.

Distribution, status and habitat conservation

Although a tropical species, this ubiquitous egret has now expanded to breed to about 45°N in both North America and Eurasia.

The race *ibis* breeds all over Africa and its islands. Avoiding the Sahara, it breeds in North Africa and southern Europe, the Middle East and patchily to the Caucasus. From here it spread to northern South America and is now expanding in suitable habitat as far south as Argentina. It moved through Central America and the Caribbean into North America where it continues to expand its range wherever suitable habitats are found. The eastern race *coromandus* extends from India eastwards as far as southeastern China, Burma, Thailand, the Philippines, and northwards to Korea and Japan. Its spread to Australia and New Zealand continues. Between these two races, a third race, *seychellarum* presents a limited 'half-way' house.

All northern birds migrate south after breeding and widespread dispersion continues. Contrary to expectation this basically dry-land feeder needs water for part of its food requirements. It feeds mainly on dry grasslands, ploughed fields and suburban lawns, generally avoiding heavily wooded areas.

Feeding

This species prospers mainly by association with mammals both large and small, other birds, tractors, indeed anything that will assist in attracting and disturbing insects or other small prey. In this way it feeds extremely efficiently. However, flooded fields, ponds and water meadows provide it with amphibians and water insects. Crickets, grasshoppers, flies, moths, bugs and indeed small mammals and birds are all taken. It usually feeds in quite large groups and roosts in ever-larger parties.

Breeding

The Cattle Egret is highly colonial and nests usually with other heron species. In new areas where sites are restricted they often crowd out local species and have thus incurred the wrath of some ornithologists who consider them a threat to 'native species'. As can be imagined, the courtship displays are noisy and aggressive. Full Forward threats, Upright Displays, Greeting Displays with all feathers raised, followed by Mutual Contact Bill Clappering are all quite spectacular.

Small twig or reed nests are built in reedbeds, bushes or trees and four to five pale green or blue eggs are laid.

The nestling bill is initially yellow, then turns gray and later becomes yellow again. This color change may be connected with sibling rivalry in receiving food from the yellow bill of the parent.

Right:
A feeding bird in nonbreeding plumage.

Below:
A nonbreeding bird of the Eastern race *coromundus*.

Below Right:
A pair of the nominate race in breeding plumage.

Above:
The eastern race has full head and neck plumes in a deep buff colour.

Above Left:
This bird in Florida has full courtship colours with bright red bills and legs.

Left:
An Indian bird on the nest showing head and full neck plumes.

Right:
The nominate race here in Spain retains a white neck in breeding plumes.

Below:
A Florida bird has a single chick.

Below Right:
This nonbreeding bird scavenges on dead animal carcasses.

Above:
All Cattle Egrets use cattle to disturb insects.

Left:
Here, in Florida, a White-tailed Deer is surrounded by feeding birds.

27
SQUACCO HERON
Ardeola ralloides

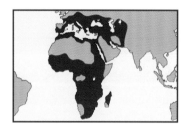

One of the well-named pond herons found throughout Europe and Africa. Like all but one of its other relatives, it changes its plumage before breeding. These pond herons look very much alike when not breeding. In flight it shows its white wings. I have watched dispersed feeding birds starting to return to their communal roost in the evening and believe their flashing wings signal each bird to 'follow my leader'.

Identification

Length: 45 cm (18 in)

The nonbreeding plumage of this heron is brown with black streaks which provides good camouflage until it flies. This heron is much more handsome when breeding, with a golden-brown breast and pale wings. The bill is blue or greenish with a black tip. Its green legs turn pink briefly during courtship.

Distribution, status and habitat conservation

The Squacco Heron is found throughout southern Europe and Africa in scattered locations. Most palearctic birds winter in North Africa. It inhabits river banks, marshes, rice fields and of course ponds, usually staying close to vegetation. Numbers are falling in many areas due to both habitat loss and pollution.

Feeding

Small fish and most other aquatic creatures are often eaten and insects are caught by Gleaning and Standing Flycatching. This declining species may use insects as lures to catch fish in the same way as the Green-backed Heron does.

Breeding

Plumes are fully erected as courtship begins. The Stretch Display includes a lateral swaying motion unlike *Ardea* or *Egretta* species; this may well be a feature of pond heron behavior. However, no interbreeding has been recorded between the otherwise quite similar pond heron species, even though their territories overlap in some areas. Pairs engage in contact Bill Clappering.

Four to six greenish-blue eggs are laid in a reed or stick nest in low bushes, papyrus or low trees. The chicks are gray, buff and white.

In breeding plumage
in papyrus beds in
the Hula Reserve in
Israel.

Right: The long crest and white wings show in flight.

Below: This bird nests colonially in mangroves in Kenya.

Below Right : A nonbreeding bird showing a striped neck.

28

INDIAN POND HERON

Ardeola grayii

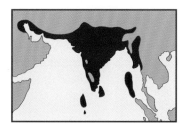

This little heron is usually intent on its fishing and will ignore you unless you become a nuisance, when it will open its white wings and leave with a disgusted squawk. It seems as though every pond in India has one.

Identification

Length: 46 cm (18 in)

The head and neck of this heron are brown with prominent buff streaks and the upper body is a dark shade of brown. The hidden wings are white and show only in flight. The underparts are white with heavy buff streaking. The bill is horn-colored with a black tip, the eye is yellow and the lores have a greenish tinge. The legs are a dull yellow.

When breeding commences things change dramatically: a dull little unobtrusive bird turns into one with long white lanceolate plumes hanging from a buff-colored nape across a deep maroon back. The underparts are white with elongated buff feathers growing from the buff-tinged breast.

The lores become blue, changing briefly to orange. The legs turn bright yellow flushing pink for a short time.

Distribution, status and habitat conservation

The Indian Pond Heron is widely distributed from the Persian Gulf across the whole Indian subcontinent, Sri Lanka and the islands of the Indian Ocean to Burma where it overlaps with both the Chinese and Japanese pond herons. This abundant bird is to be found where either fresh or salty ponds occur.

Feeding

The species Stands or Walks Slowly, crouching down to thrust its bill forward. I have seen it hover above water to capture insects. While small fish such as mudskippers are its favorite diet, it will, like most heron species, eat frogs, crabs and all sorts of insects.

Breeding

Apart from the fanning of feathers displaying its maroon mantle, little is known of its courtship display. They nest in mixed colonies, in small groups or singly. The nest, a roughly-constructed pad of twigs, is built in all sorts of vegetation, such as trees and bushes.

They lay dark blue-green eggs, usually numbering three to six. Surprisingly, little is known about incubation or feeding of the young. Also surprising is their choice of nesting site: although common at Bharatpur, they seldom nest within the boundaries of the great colonies of egrets there and prefer to use trees some way from the reserve.

Feeding birds crouch low for long periods awaiting prey.

Above Left:
In breeding colors.

Above :
In flight the white
wings become
prominent.

Left:
Fish are among a
large selection of
prey caught by this
adaptable species.

29
CHINESE POND HERON

Ardeola bacchus

Feeding in Chinese rice paddies is a hazardous venture and this brightly colored species has a much less benign time than its Indian relative. The decline of the safe-haven Buddhist sanctuaries in recent times has not helped either. I traveled a very long distance in southern China before I found one, although claims are made that it is quite common in some areas.

Identification

Length: 45 cm (18 in)

In nonbreeding plumage, this pond heron is extremely hard to separate from the other wintering members of this genus. Three species – the Chinese, Indian and Japanese birds – are sometimes found together in the marshes of Bangkok and I have spent many hours trying to differentiate between them. However, its Latin name *bacchus*, after the God of Wine, well describes its deep wine-colored head and chest. Beneath, it is all-white, including the chin. The back is a slaty or purplish color. Long lanceolate plumes trail from the nape. The bill is yellow with a dark tip and the lores are greenish-yellow. The iris too is yellow.

Immature birds are similar with heavy brown buff streaks but showing more white beneath.

Distribution, status and habitat conservation

Like all pond herons, it inhabits marshes, ponds, rice fields and river margins. Distributed patchily in northern and eastern China, this species used to be considered one of the commonest herons in this country. It winters well to the south in Malay, Borneo and Thailand. Some birds wander to Japan and Taiwan after breeding.

Feeding

While feeding in marshes, and even in torrents at quite high altitude, this heron also seems content to feed in much dryer grasslands than its relatives.

Unlike the Indian Pond Heron, the Chinese Pond Heron's human neighbors are not so tolerant and thus it is forced to be more secretive, feeding early or late in the day. It eats the usual diet of fish, reptiles and crustaceans.

Breeding

The presentation of a stick to a mate is the only form of display recorded so far. When nesting in colonies with other heron species it occupies a low position in the trees, but is quite near the top when singly or in its own group. In protected ornamental gardens in China it will nest in bamboo thickets, quite close to human habitation. A simple twig nest holds three to five greenish blue eggs.

In breeding plumes this species has a dark vinal colored head and neck. Hence its Latin name *Bacchus*.

30
JAVANESE POND HERON

Ardeola speciosa

The fact that this little heron is also found outside Java will almost certainly have saved it from extinction. The quite extraordinary deliberate destruction of forest areas across hundreds of thousands of hectares by fires lit for land clearance by the larger landowners will wipe out many creatures. Certainly this so-called 'Tiger' economy will pay dearly for its greed. This enormous act of sheer vandalism will have far-reaching effects on the whole region's ecosystem.

Identification

Length: 45 cm (18 in)

The nondescript brown-streaked plumage of this heron gives way, when the breeding season approaches, to a bird almost identical to the Chinese Pond Heron apart from the golden yellow color of the head and neck.

Distribution, status and habitat conservation

Formerly quite common throughout its range; it was found in southeast Burma, Borneo, Indonesia and some of the islands to the east. It was once a common bird in Vietnam and Cambodia.

This species inhabits areas which for many years have been subjected to very heavy habitat destruction as well as the continual warfare raging in some areas. Over 30 years ago I found it prospering on the Indonesian island of Pular Dua, but throughout this region nest destruction by fishermen, heavy pollution and increased movements of people have wreaked havoc with this population.

Wherever possible it inhabits mangroves, grasslands, rice fields and the margins of ponds and lakes.

Feeding

The Javanese Pond Heron may sometimes feed in groups, enjoying the same diet as the other members of this broadly similar genus.

Breeding

The four very similar pond herons, while alike in behavior, appear not to interbreed. Presumably, in addition to color differences in breeding plumes, other courtship displays as yet unreported prevent interbreeding.

The twig nest contains the usual three to five greenish-blue eggs, and is generally placed among other heron species in mixed colonies, or occasionally on its own.

A bird in breeding plumage. The wings are darker than the Squacco or Indian birds.

31

MALAGASY POND HERON

Ardeola idea

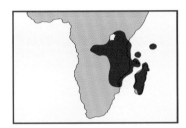

This small heron, like much of the endemic wildlife of this large offshore African island, is not doing very well. Perhaps the arrival of its African mainland counterpart or the inevitable forest destruction have caused its numbers to fall dramatically. In common with nearly all emerging peoples, those of Madagascar sadly are driven to clearing trees for agriculture and fuel wood.

Identification

Length: 45 cm (17–18 in)

While the nonbreeding plumes make the Malagasy Pond Heron hard to distinguish from its neighbor the Squacco Heron, its breeding plumage sets it apart from all its close relatives in this genus. It becomes completely white with dense nuptial plumes on the crown and nape, back, fore-neck and breast. The bill changes from yellow to deep blue, but retains a black tip. The dull yellow legs turn pink.

Distribution, status and habitat conservation

This species breeds only on Madagascar and Aldabra, but winters on the African mainland. A few dispersals to the Seychelles and the Comoro Islands may hold out the possibility of it extending its range, but meanwhile the bird is coming under great pressure on its native Madagascar. It inhabits marshes, swamps, lakes and ponds, and in winter forages on quite open ground.

Feeding

Fish are eaten but amphibians and aquatic insects also form a large part of the diet. It hunts its prey by Walking Slowly and flies up to trees when disturbed.

Breeding

The use of the wings in aggressive displays and probably in courtship is the only written description of this heron's breeding displays.

A large twig nest is built in tall trees or small bushes depending on their availability. The eggs are pale greenish-white and two to four are laid. The chicks are covered in a thick buffy-yellow down and are thus easily distinguished from the neighboring Squaccos.

A nonbreeding bird. The stripes are darker and thicker than other members of this family.

32

RUFOUS-BELLIED HERON

Ardeola rufiventris

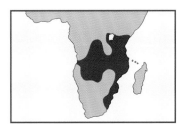

This small, dark gray heron with its rufous front does not change to a striped, camouflaged plumage like other pond herons when not breeding. The taxonomists are concerned about this lack of typical dimorphism and argue over whether it should really be classified with the pond herons.

Identification

Length: 39 cm (15 in)

The male bird is dark gray with chestnut-red shoulder patches, belly, rump and tail. The bill is horn-colored with a brown tip and the legs are yellow, as is the iris. Uniquely for this group, the female differs in its plumage. The main plumes are duller and browner, and there is a buffy-white streak from the chin to the foreneck. The lores are pale (almost white), and the bill greenish but with a dark tip.

The immature bird shows some streaking of a buff-brown color on the head, neck and upper breast. During courtship the iris turns orange, as do the toes.

Distribution, status and habitat conservation

The vast swamps of the Kagera river between Tanzania and Rwanda may hold the largest concentration of this heron. In Zambia, also, on Lake Bangwulu, up to 80 nests have been recorded. It is present in the Okavango delta, Botswana, and occurs in Cape Province, South Africa, but is rare northwards in Central and East Africa. Migration or dispersal occurs after breeding.

It inhabits dense reedbeds, grassy wetlands and the borders of lakes and rivers.

Feeding

Either alone or in small groups, this bird often feeds with Squacco Herons and other small wading birds, such as Black-winged Stilts *Himantopus himantopus*.

It assumes the Crouched Posture and Walks Slowly often freezing, bittern-like, but with bill horizontal when disturbed.

Breeding

Rainfall triggers breeding. This species nests colonially, often with other herons and storks. The nest is built of twigs, with a pad of reed stems, usually in the fork of a tree. Two to four pale blue eggs are laid. Predation by the Black Crake *Amaurornis flavirostra* is common.

This dark-plumed bird does not change plumes from nonbreeding to breeding as all the other pond herons do.

33

GREEN-BACKED HERON

Butorides striatus

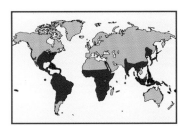

This widespread little character has given Europe a miss. It is found everywhere else, although its plumage variations from place to place cause confusion and each country in turn claims that their race is really a separate species. (It is the habitat that does it.) On a volcanic island such as the Galapagos Islands, it is nearly black. In Australia it blends in with the muddy shoreline of the tidal rivers. In northern America its rich coloration blends with the multicolored foliage in which it lives. There are, quite unbelievably, more than 30 subspecies around the globe

Identification

Length: 40 cm (16 in)

Each of the many recognized races of this wide-ranging little bird has a plumage adapted to suit its environment. Many of the races are grayish-green with a pale gray neck. The crown can be dark green or black and the edge of the wing feathers have a pale margin. The short legs range from yellow, brown to pink according to season. The bill too has a similar color range.

As usual, immature birds are duller generally.

Distribution, status and habitat conservation

The heron is widespread throughout the Americas, as far north as the Great Lakes and southwards to Chile and the Argentine. It is found in all of Africa south of the Sahara, the Gulf coasts, the Indian subcontinent, most of the rest of Asia, parts of China to the east and Japan. It is even found along Australia's northern and eastern coastlines and in Tasmania. Although some migration from the north takes place, it is often a sedentary species. However, after breeding, widespread dispersal is quite common and it is probably this which results in colonization of islands over a wide area.

It frequents both fresh and salt water, however small the patch of suitable habitat may be.

Feeding

This highly energetic little bird feeds by Standing in a Crouching position, but all other known methods of feeding are adopted to meet the prevailing circumstances. Flycatching, Head Swaying, Neck Swaying, Foot Stirring, and Foot Raking are only some of its strategies. It will Jump, Plunge, Swim Feed and, cleverest of all, present bait to attract fish, dropping an insect or piece of vegetation onto the water surface and waiting for a fish to rise. I strongly suspect it learned this trick watching fish being fed in zoos or private fisheries and quickly imitated it successfully.

It eats fish, insects, amphibians, crabs, prawns and most other aquatic life of an appropriate size.

Breeding

As would be expected, the courtship ritual is quite distinctive, involving much Crest Raising followed by Aerial displays. Circle Flights, 'Crooked-neck' Flights and Snap Displays are accompanied by frequent calls, usually a harsh rasp. It also constantly flicks its tail up and down.

Nesting is solitary or in loose colonies. The nest is a flimsy platform of twigs, placed in a low bush or tree. Two to four pale-green eggs, but sometimes as many as seven, are laid

Right:
This young bird still
has a brown back.

Middle :
This highly acrobatic
bird uses a ship's
rope as a perch to
catch a fish.

Below:
An adult of
the race *viviscens* in
Florida, USA, as are
the two above.

Above Right:
The West Indian race in Tobago. *Immaculatus* has a paler neck color than *viviscens*.

Above Left:
This young viviscens is coming into full adult plumage; the bright chestnut feathering on the neck are newly acquired.

Left:
The neck color of this West African race *atricapillus* is gray with a faint darker stripe.

Above:

The blue grey back of the race *viviscens* acts as camouflage when feeding.

Right:

The northern Australian race *stagnatalis* blends into the muddy bank of the South Alligator river.

34
AGAMI HERON
Agamia agami

We do not know as much about this weird long-billed, long-necked bird as we should. The literature maintains that it is rarely seen, but in many places it is quite common. All this probably means is that observers, rather than the birds, are thin on the ground.

Identification

Length: Up to 76 cm (30 in), the average is slightly smaller

This heron is bottle-green above, chestnut below, with a white border on the throat and neck. The face and crown are black. The neck is very long and the bill can reach more than 18 cm (7 in) long. It also has very short legs which makes for a most unusual-shaped bird. This could well be an adaptation to feed from a bank down into water, which it does most often, usually from within thick foliage.

The bill and lores are pale yellow and the legs olive green. The iris is orange-colored. It would appear that the bill becomes blue with a black tip and this, together with brightening of the legs, could indicate the start of breeding. Similarly, bluish-white crest feathers develop and broad slate-blue plumes grow from the back. It is a quite unforgettable species if you are fortunate enough to see it.

Distribution, status and habitat conservation

The Agami Heron is found over most of Central America and down the western coastal strip of South America. It is considered common in Panama, at least between January and June. It is seldom seen in central and eastern South America but is found along the Rio Jurua in western Brazil. It is not recorded further south.

Regular migration may take place but certainly odd reports from Trinidad indicate some movement probably to and from Venezuela or Colombia, and at least one nest has been found there. Its preferred habitat is a small watercourse in thick forest.

Feeding

Fish appear to make up the bulk of the diet and the thick lance-like bill and long neck enable the bird to spear them from the bank rather than by wading.

Breeding

This heron's courtship display remains to be recorded, and it can only be postulated that the long serpent-like neck comes into play.

The Agami is often, but not always, a colonial nester. Quite deep twig or stick nests are built in trees or mangrove bushes. The eggs are pale bluish-brown and from two to as many as six are laid.

The brightly colored Agami Heron uses its long neck and bill to spear fish while standing on a river bank.

35

YELLOW-CROWNED NIGHT HERON

Nycticorax violaceus

(or Nyctanassa)

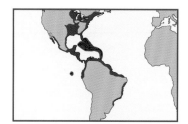

This highly-specialized night heron perhaps deserves to be in its own special genus. It has large eyes to help it feed at dusk and dawn but, where it is not threatened, it feeds all day. Again, while it is extremely shy at the nest, it will appear quite tame when feeding in some areas.

After its numbers fell dramatically during the plume-hunting years, its recovery has been spectacular and it has extended its breeding range northwards into Canada.

Identification

Length: 55–70 cm (22–28 in)

The Yellow-crowned Night Heron does not retract its neck so it looks quite tall and upright. Its head is black with a white crown, crest and cheek patches. The body is gray with darker gray, wiry feathers edged with lighter gray. The white crown turns yellow soon after molting, giving it its name. The bill is black, often with a yellow base on the lower mandible and this turns shiny green during courtship. At this time the gray lores turn bright green. The eye is scarlet and the legs yellow, but these also turn bright red at the start of the breeding season. The head plumes are white and grow quite long. When flying, the legs extend well behind the wings.

Immature birds are already brown in their first year and in the second are gray with indistinct markings. It is not until the third year that they acquire adult plumes.

There are four other races of this species. *Pauper* is found in the Galapagos and *bancrofti* is found in Baja California, the Central American Pacific coast as far Guatemala and all the West Indies south to Tobago. The darker *cayennsis* occupies the north and east coast of South America while *caliginis* ranges south from Panama along the Pacific coast to Peru. Because these local races are joined by migrants from the north, field identification is very difficult indeed.

Distribution, status and habitat conservation

The Yellow-crowned Night Heron is a specialized feeder but its expanding range has necessitated its adaptation to a wider diet. It finds this in a very wide variety of habitats from swamps and mangroves to tidal mudflats, rock shores, riverbanks, ponds and reservoirs and, on small islands, in thicketed or arid terrain. It inhabits parklands, suburban estates or wild forest swamps.

Feeding

This species is indeed a crab-eater *par excellence*. In Tobago I have watched it remain silent and upright, not moving at all above a crab hole until its prey emerges and is then quickly snapped up. Small crabs are quickly swallowed but larger crabs take some time to be dissected by the powerful bill.

Fish, eels especially, frogs and other small amphibians and mammals, young birds, snakes and reptiles are among the many other prey of this heron.

Breeding

Considerable numbers of Circle Flights as well as Crest Raising, Bill Clappering and Stretch Displays, form part of the courtship ritual.

Nests are strongly built of twigs sometimes lined with grass. They are usually in tall trees, but have been discovered on lava ledges or on the bare floor of a cave. Where nesting is in colonies, the nests are well spread out. In my experience, most nests are well hidden but, if discovered, the sitting bird will raise its feathers in a bittern-like display.

Above:
First-year birds have small white specks on their dark brown plumage. The speckles on the similar colored Black Crowned juvenile bird are somewhat larger and more elongated.

Left:
The legs and feet extend back beyond the tail when flying.

Above :

Fully adult birds feeding largely on crabs which they may have to break with their strong bills before swallowing.

Above Right:

Young birds do not acquire their white neck colours until they are 2 years old.

Right:

The large red eyes are used in night feeding, although in undisturbed areas it will feed all day.

36

BLACK-CROWNED NIGHT HERON

Nycticorax nycticorax

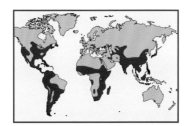

You might find this widespread bird anywhere in the world except in Australia. It is very aggressive and is disliked by all other herons, whose frequent attacks upon it have forced it over the centuries to become a night-time feeder. When breeding it will steal eggs and young in the colony in which it breeds, hence its unpopularity

Identification

Length: 58–65 cm (23–26 in)

In adult plumage this is a handsome bird. It is gray and white with a jet-black head and a thin white line extending from the forehead and above the large red eyes. The back is black and two or three thin, long white plumes extend down it from the nape. The bill is black and slightly curved. The lores are dark green, and the legs and feet yellow. These become red during courtship and the black plumage takes on a gloss. With such a wide range it can necessarily be divided into several races but none of these allow recognition since the differences are small.

Immature birds have a brown-streaked plumage which darkens and becomes more prominent with age until the molt to full adulthood occurs. Its numerous and varied vocal calls have been the subject of many curious written descriptions (of rather dubious value).

Distribution, status and habitat conservation

A very abundant and widely distributed species. It is found in much of North, Central and South America, and is patchily distributed in much of Europe with particularly large colonies in northern Italy. In Africa, a few colonies exist in the north but many more occur south of the Sahara, as far south as Cape Town, but never in deserts or dense jungle.

Throughout the Middle East distribution is also patchy, but it is commoner on the Indian subcontinent. It is well distributed through East Asia and northwards to Japan. It disperses widely and thus can be seen well away from its normal range. It migrates into Africa from Europe and makes north–south movements in Asia, as well as in the Americas.

It can be found almost anywhere, even in the suburbs of quite large cities, provided that trees for roosting and nesting are available.

Feeding

I have watched birds from a colony take off to rob tern chicks on an island off Oahu, in the Hawaiian islands. Robbing of nests is rampant wherever it inhabits mixed heron colonies.

This species prefers to feed at night because if it ventures abroad in daylight it will be subjected to attacks from all other feeding birds. It is described as an opportunistic general feeder, taking any available prey and a wide range of feeding behavior is reported. Perhaps rice fields can be considered the most attractive areas and their proliferation in Italy has resulted in rapidly increasing numbers there.

Breeding

Fully adult at the age of 3 years when breeding plumes are displayed, pair formation involves Mock Preening, Bill Clapper, Bow and Wing Touch among a number of other displays.

Nests can be placed in trees, bushes, on rocks, grassy tussocks or reeds in mixed or single colonies. Young birds build a fragile, twig nest, but reuse over the years creates quite a bulky platform. Three to five pale blue-green eggs are laid.

Left:

This bird is building a nest deep in the mangroves in South Florida. It's legs are pink not red.

Below Left :

The race *hoactli* breeds throughout the new world. It's white eye streak is narrow. It is larger than the nominate race.

Below Right:

This immature bird has prominent white markings on its brown plumage. The hunched back and slightly curved bill are well illustrated.

Above:

This race *nycticorae* has much darker legs when in breeding plumage, here in Indonesia.

Above Right:

In South-East Asia the eye stripe is wider.

Right:

The pale white wings of this hovering bird are very conspicuous.

Both adult and immature birds share a day roost here in India.

The Falkland Island race shown here is darker than the other races, and also has a light phase. It is a smaller bird than those on the mainlands.

37
NANKEEN NIGHT HERON

Nycticorax caledonicus

Where this heron overlaps with its Black-crowned cousin around the islands north of Australia it will, at times, interbreed. While it is a very different color and is accepted as a separate species, it is apparent that the two species have been separated for only a few million years.

Identification

Length: 59 cm (23 in)

This species has the shape and appearance of the Black-crowned Night Heron but apart from a similar black head and white plumes, the colors are very different. The Australians, in whose land this bird has its major home, call it 'Rufous'. This describes the pale color of the foreneck and upper breast and the deep chestnut upperparts. The underparts are white. The bill is large and decurved, usually black with some green, blending into the green of the lores. The eye is yellow and the legs a greenish yellow, both becoming pink or red during the breeding season.

The immature bird matches the color and appearance of the Black-crowned and cannot easily be told apart.

No less than five races are recognized, although the differences are not great.

Distribution, status and habitat conservation

A common bird throughout Australia, although seldom moving to the center. It is found in New Caledonia, Java, New Guinea and is common in the Philippines, although probably only as a visitor, with a few birds known to have interbred with Black-crowns. This species is inclined to wander but no migratory pattern has been established. It prefers swamps and flooded grasslands near trees. In winter roosts are sometimes very large and occur even in the center of cities such as Melbourne and Adelaide where they congregate in the zoological gardens. Less benign authorities in Perth destroyed them there because they raided the goldfish pond.

Feeding

The Nankeen Heron hunts mainly by night, except when raising young. It has exactly the same diet as the Black-crowned Night Heron and has the same habit of plundering other birds' nests for young or eggs.

Breeding

Little is known of its courtship behavior. Mainly nesting colonially, this species builds a loose, stick nest in a tree or mangrove bush. It has nested, when on an undisturbed island, either under vegetation or on bare ground. The two to three eggs laid are pale greenish-blue.

Nonbreeding adult.

This race, *hilli*, is found in most of Australia.

38

WHITE-BACKED NIGHT HERON

Nycticorax leuconotus

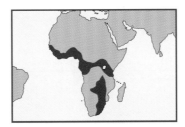

Lots of people watch birds in Africa but few ever see this one. It lives in reedbeds like a bittern and its large eye aids its night-time activities. It probably migrates during the rainy season.

Identification

Length: 50–55 cm (21 in)

A wide circle of white around the large red eye with a black head, nape and thick crest, immediately identify this shy species. It has a white chin and deep rufous neck, the upperparts are dark brown and beneath the belly is patterned buff and light brown. The bill is black and very slightly decurved. The lores are green with a pale chestnut patch in front of the eye. The legs are yellow. The soft-parts as usual brighten, with legs turning orange and the eye deep red.

Immature birds have buff-brown, speckled breasts and upperparts, but are more heavily spotted on the wings and back.

Distribution, status and habitat conservation

This is an African species found south of the Sahara but quite patchily distributed, avoiding heavy jungle and desert. A swampland bird of very dense vegetation, it is hard to see and thus details of its distribution are scarce, particularly as it invariably retreats to cover by day.

Feeding

Few firm details have emerged of the diet or feeding behavior of this species, although two captive chicks were successfully reared on small fish.

Breeding

As one would expect no displays have been observed.

Bulky nests of twigs have been discovered in trees overhanging water. There are reports of a nest built on a rock in a river and of some in reedbeds. Green-white eggs, up to five in number, have been recorded.

The white ring around the eye is conspicuous in this very crepuscular African species.

39

WHITE-EARED NIGHT HERON

Gorsachius magnificus

As far as we can tell the last record of this bird was from Tienmu in Chekiang in north-eastern China. Early collectors took specimens from various parts of eastern China. The most dramatic of these was from Five Finger Mountain on the island of Hainan by John Whitehead, who died before reaching home. I talked to Dr Cheng Tso-Hsin on a visit to the Academia Sinica in Beijing. He said it had once bred on Hainan Island but that he hadn't seen it himself. The Chinese would not let me go there so all I saw was a stuffed specimen into the bill of which someone had inserted a fish.

Identification

Length: 54 cm (21–22 in)

This night heron is certainly a magnificent-looking bird, as its Latin name implies, but it only appears at night so has rarely been seen. It has dark gray-brown upperparts which are tinged with purple. Yellow orange on the side of the neck merges with brown on the back. The underside is mottled with brown-edged white feathers. The distinctive pattern of the head gives it its common name. The brown head with short neck plumes is divided by a broad white eye-stripe and the chin and upper neck are white. The large eye is pale yellow and the bill brown with yellow-green on the lower mandible. The legs are quite a bright green.

The female coloring is less prominent with a shorter crest. The juvenile has no crest with an altogether browner, more mottled plumage.

A description taken solely from museum skins cannot fully capture the true coloring of the living bird and it may well be that this scarce species is even more colorful than specimens would indicate.

Distribution, status and habitat conservation

This heron is confined to a very small area of eastern China but is also found on the mountains of the island of Hainan. While many think that this night heron migrates between these two widely separated areas, wintering only in Hainan, the Chinese believe that it also nests in the high tropical area of Hainan.

It has been found in densely forested well-watered areas, including bamboo zones. In China, as elsewhere, these habitats are under enormous development pressure.

Feeding and breeding

It appears to feed on the ground and retreat to the top of tall trees when disturbed. Nests are thought to be placed either in pine or bamboo, but none have so far been found. As yet, we know nothing of its diet or its nesting behavior: the fish in the mouth of the museum specimen photographed here seems somewhat incongruous.

Above:
Having been refused
permission to seek
out this species in
Hainan, I was shown
a museum specimen
in the Academia
Sinica in Beijing.
It is doubtful if the
fish stuck in its
mouth is really an
item of its diet.

Left:
This rare Chinese
species is seldom
seen.

40
JAPANESE NIGHT HERON

Gorsachius goisagi

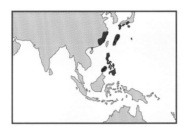

Well south of Tokyo and away from the city smog, this small heron feeds early in the day and then again when night falls. They say it is quite tame, but perhaps only when in company with other wintering birds in the Philippines.

Identification

Length: 49 cm (19 in)

This is one of the three night herons of Asia, all of which have much shorter bills than the other night herons.

This one is a small chestnut-brown bird. The head and neck are light chestnut. The chin and neck are pale buff with speckles above and darker streaks stretching along the belly. The upper parts are a dull brown. The primaries are blackish. Its eye is yellow, as are the lores. The short bill is brown above and yellow below. The legs and feet are dark green. The bill turns blue during breeding.

The immature bird is spottier, streakier, paler and even less distinguishable than the adult.

Distribution, status and habitat conservation

Found only in the less crowded areas on the Japanese mainland, this heron migrates south with many other heron species to south-eastern China, Taiwan, the Philippines, the Palau Islands and north Sulaweri. It is not a common bird and recent sightings in these areas are few.

Feeding

The diet is mainly of small crabs, insects and perhaps some fish. Feeding mainly takes place at night or early in the morning.

Breeding

No courtship behavior is known.

Nesting is usually solitary but sometimes small, well-spaced-out nests have been found in loose groups. Crude stick nests have been found mainly in conifers. Three to four dull-white eggs make up the clutch.

Robert Gillmar

A shy inconspicuous little heron seldom seen by day.

41

MALAYAN NIGHT HERON

Gorsachius melanolophus

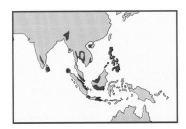

Scattered about in Asia, this short-billed heron heads south in winter. The birds from western India migrate to Sri Lanka, others head eastwards to the islands of South-East Asia. Lighthouses along the way report many birds killed or injured on their night-time passage

Identification

Length: 49 cm (19 in)

The back and wing coverts of this heron are chestnut with thin bars of black. The crown and nape are black with a long black crest. The tail is also black. The chin, throat and belly are white with speckled and brown streaks and the face and neck are rufous. The bill is slightly larger than its congeners, but can still be described as stocky and it turns downwards at the tip. It is dark brown or greenish and the lores are also green. The eye is yellow and, again, not as noticeably large as others of this genus. The legs are dull yellow. Both lores and legs turn pink during courtship.

The immature bird is barred and mottled brown and black, with a blackish crown, streaked with a buffish-white. These birds are barely distinguished from the young of the Black-crowned Night Heron, except for the stubbier bill.

Distribution, status and habitat conservation

The Malayan Night Heron has quite a wide distribution from India through South-East Asia to as far as the Philippines. Stragglers are even reported from Hainan, China; it certainly still nests in Thailand and Indo-China. It lives in subtropical forests, and appears to be present in quite good numbers in its somewhat disjointed range.

This species migrates southwards in winter, flying at night, although except for the quite well understood movement of the two populations of Indian birds, its journeys are not well documented.

Feeding

Its diet consists mainly of insects, lizards, frogs and possibly small fish caught at night. It is, however, seen in isolated nullah pools on quiet hilltops in Indian daylight hours, if not disturbed. Otherwise rice fields or, in Borneo, vegetable gardens, are its main feeding grounds.

Breeding

Small stick nests are placed in low trees sometimes in loose colonies, sometimes in reeds, but always well hidden. Quite large chalky-white eggs are laid in clutches of four or five.

This small heron breeds in hill tracts in India and in parts of South-East Asia.

42
BOAT-BILLED HERON

Cochlearius cochlearius

This species very deservedly receives special taxonomic treatment. While it feeds like other herons it can also scoop up food with its wide bill. It Bill Clappers like other species but also has a range of variable chanting calls, echoed in chorus by others nearby. When disturbed it raises its crest in annoyance before retreating into the bushes.

Identification

Length: 45–51 cm (18–20 in)

The extraordinary broad, thick bill distinguishes this bird from all other heron species. It has a black cap and a white forehead and cheeks. The wings are pale gray and the upper back is black with the remainder gray. The underparts are a deep rufous color with the flanks black. The tibia has heavy feathering which is also black. The bill is black with a distinctive yellow tip. The eyes are dusky with a yellow eyelid. The legs are a dull green or gray. The gular pouch, when distended, is yellow or gray or, in Brazil, pink.

Males have long, black occipital plumes which extend fan-like in a spectacular display.

Immature birds go through a series of molts before achieving adult plumage, starting with dull rufous backs and wings, and dingy white below.

It adopts a hunched-back position with bill lowered when resting.

Distribution, status and habitat conservation

Several quite distinct populations are found ranging from the coasts of north Central Mexico south to Peru, Bolivia and north-eastern Argentina. — This species appears to be mainly sedentary, inhabiting freshwater creeks, mangrove-covered tidal flats and lakes surrounded by thick bushes. It likes to nest and roost over, or at least close to, water.

Feeding

While feeding, generally, the Boat-billed Heron Walks Slowly, scooping prey into its large bill. It will also Walk Quickly, dashing about, then stopping abruptly. Its Scooping action is often used with the bill partly submerged in mud or leaf litter. Its diet includes shrimps, fish and insects.

It roosts while awaiting the tide along the coast, both by day and night.

Breeding

This unique species also has a unique set of courtship displays. It uses its Crest Raised movement extensively and also Tail Rocks, moving slowly from side to side. A Wings Out position is given on landing and pairs engage in both Contact and Non-contact Bill Clappering. Short and Long Chants with a background chorus from other birds is a unique feature of this species.

Small nests are built quite openly in small bushes, solitarily, in groups or in mixed colonies. Two to four pale blue eggs are laid. Chicks are fed only at night while they are young. They resemble ducklings with thick down, a black crown, yellow skin and pale gray above.

A pair of breeding birds in Brazil. The smaller female has a partly rufous crown and may well be a semi-adult. The long crest of the male develops before nesting begins.

The male's crest is raised when disturbed and during other displays.

Resting Boat-bills adopt a typical hunched posture.

43

BARE-THROATED
TIGER HERON

Tigrisoma mexicanum

A handsome, though darkly-plumed heron, this Central American bird is, on occasions, less cautious than the other tiger herons. It has a habit of sitting boldly on tree stumps quite high over the water. When breeding, its bare throat becomes bright orange-yellow. Despite this occasional flamboyant behavior, it seems to survive predation and disturbance quite well.

Identification

Length: 71–81 cm (28–32 in)

This is quite a large, striking-looking bird, as indeed are all the tiger herons. Its appearance superficially resembles a bittern and it has often been described as such. The crown and nape are black and the cheeks gray. A black line stretching from the eye separates the black-streaked white chin from the upper neck. This in turn blends into the dusky brown upperparts. The throat is pale, streaky-buff surrounding a bare apple-green skin which gives its name. The long bill is black with a green base. The eye is yellow and the legs dark green. When breeding commences the bare skin of the throat turns bright yellow or orange.

The immature bird is heavily barred and spotted with cinnamon-buff and brown. The tail and wings are darker with thin, white bars across.

Much snorting, booming and barking occurs, particularly at the nest.

Distribution, status and habitat conservation

A resident species in mangroves, marshes and swamps, this heron's range extends from Mexico south through most of Central America into northern Columbia. In the Sonova and Sinaloa states of Mexico up to altitudes of 440 m (1444 feet). It also inhabits freshwater rivers and streams.

Feeding

The Bare-throated Tiger Heron feeds alone or in small, loose groups. It catches fish, frogs or crustaceans with a quick jab from a Standing position. It uses foliage to remain hidden but does not appear to be shy.

Breeding

A courtship dance described as pair bonding is carried out by both birds facing each other with necks and bodies horizontal and feathers erect. Bill and neck are then raised vertically by one bird as it advances and the other then mimics this movement. Three hoarse booms signal a slight withdrawal. This performance can be repeated four or five times. Other displays involve rhythmic swaying of the neck from a crouched posture, or bittern-like postures repeated by each bird in turn. Croaking calls continue but can also be used at other times. Booming and barking can be heard throughout the year.

Large, sometimes poorly constructed nests are placed on a horizontal bough up to 15 m (50 feet) above running water, although in Panama they were in low overhanging branches over a cliff edge by the sea. We have recently learned that in Guatemala this bird nests on the cliffs themselves. Given the large number of avian predators in cliff habitats this seems to be living unduly dangerously.

The eggs are plain dull white with perhaps a faint greenish tinge or with buff dots. One, two or three eggs are laid. The nestling has gray down with a white crown.

Above:
Although a dull-plumed species, its bright yellow green bare throat is most distinctive.

Above Right:
The well-patterned young bird becomes less well marked when adult.

Right:
An adult sitting on its large stick nest in Mexico.

44

FASCIATED TIGER HERON

Tigrisoma fasciatum

Fast-flowing mountain streams within tropical forests are not as abundant as they once were in either Central or South America and this smallest of the tiger herons stays in such preferred habitat all year round. Like its shrinking habitat, it forms a relic population of several varying races

Identification

Length: 66 cm (26 in)

The Fasciated Tiger Heron is the smallest of the tiger herons and has quite a dark brown plumage with closely spaced buff bars across it. The foreneck and breast are white with dark brown streaks. The underbelly is a pale rufous color. The under-wing coverts are partially barred, slaty and white. The strong bill is slightly curved and varies in color from horn at the tip to blackish above, the lower mandible being yellow. This pattern appears to alter with age. The lores too appear variable from black, bordering yellow to quite bright yellow. The iris is yellow and the legs dusky brown, often dull green behind. The three described races are hard to separate in the field.

The immature birds are much paler and whiter.

Distribution, status and habitat conservation

Probably a quite widespread species at one time, this heron appears to have survived in suitable habitat in small areas stretching from the Caribbean slope of Costa Rica and Panama, south to Bolivia, northern Argentina and south-eastern Brazil.

It inhabits montane districts with wet tropical forests that have fast-flowing streams and, while it overlaps both the Bare-throated and Rufescent species, its somewhat distinctive habitat assures separation.

Feeding

A solitary feeder, this species Walks Slowly along banks of fast-flowing streams or fishes from midstream rocks. It eats fish and aquatic insects. Most of its hunting is probably done at night but if undisturbed it may venture out in the daytime.

Breeding

Virtually nothing is known of the behavior or biology of this species.

This seldom seen heron is patchly distributed in a few places in Central and South America.

45

RUFESCENT TIGER HERON

Tigrisoma lineatum

The few observations of this heron nearly all date from several decades ago, so I was surprised to find its abundant presence well south of its supposed range. It also surprised me with its calm, almost indifferent attitude towards my intrusion, even more surprising it completely ignored a guacho in his wide-brimmed hat as he trotted on his horse beneath its nest. In fact, the only time I saw one get excited was when some Whistling Herons tried to muscle in on its feeding territory, and that was soon over.

Identification

Length: 66–76 cm (26–30 in)

The most highly colored of its genus, the Rufescent Tiger Heron is distinguished by its strong rufous-colored head and neck. The foreneck is feathered white with prominent reddish brown streaks down its full length. The upperparts are dark, flecked with brown. The abdomen is gray and the underwing coverts slaty with white banding. The bill varies according to age and season, from horn green to black and the lores are yellow. The eye is yellow and the legs are horn with green sides. During courtship the eye turns bright red and the lores at the base of the bill also brighten.

The immature plumage changes to full adult plumage over the first 2 or 3 years and perhaps as long as 5 years. The buff barred-brown becomes bolder with black spots on the breast. The chestnut color makes its appearance halfway through its second year.

Distribution, status and habitat conservation

From southern Mexico this widespread species range extends through Central America and virtually the whole of South America west of the Andes to as far south as northern Argentina. West of the Andes it reaches only to Ecuador.

Its habitat is swamp, marsh and slow-moving rivers inland and mangroves on the coast. It requires water fringed with woodland for nesting and also occupies hilly country. Certainly common in suitable habitat, I have seen it well south of its previously reported range in some numbers.

Feeding

This bird feeds by Standing either on a bank or floating vegetation. The long neck and bill are used to strike with lightning speed. Fish and aquatic insects are its main diet. It is quite aggressive territorially and I have seen it drive off Whistling Herons that ventured too close.

Breeding

A large stick nest is built high up on the branch of a tall tree. Some nests are reported as being roughly built or quite flimsy. Only one or two off-white and faintly-marked eggs are laid, and I found a chick newly hatched in white down, together with an addled egg.

Above Left:
This nest was in an Argentinian marshland.

Above Right:
The sitting bird adopts a bittern-like posture.

Left:
The chick is newly hatched with white down.

Above:

As the sun begins to shine on the nest later in the day, the chick is sheltered by the adult.

Right:

Only one of the two pale eggs hatched. The other was addled.

Above:
The chick shows pale tufted down and the bill is long and yellow.

Left:
This captive bird raises its crest as it sits on eggs on the ground.

This pair of birds were brooding eggs at a near by nest in Peru. When not at the nest the 'off-duty' bird used this same tree in which to rest. One of this breeding pair shows distinctive speckling on the crown and nape. Whether this indicates sexual dimorphism, or that one of the pair has not reached full maturity, it is not possible to tell.

As can be seen from the quite distinctive plumage of the two year bird overleaf (on page 200), such plumages continue to change for up to five years in this species.

Tiger herons take some years before they have full adult plumage.
This immature bird is about 2 years old.

46

NEW GUINEA TIGER HERON

Zonerodius heliosylus

This highly obscure bird has a very limited range but survives because it takes a great deal of trouble to avoid the human race and, in view of our behavior, it must be considered most wise. We think it only feeds at night, but we know its plumage is arranged to give maximum camouflage in the shadowy, heavily forested waterholes where it lives.

Identification

Length: 71 cm (28 in)

A black head tops a completely speckled, light and dark brown neck and body. Its chin and under belly, however, are white. A long dark bill, yellow lores and eye, together with legs that are yellow or dusky brown, completes the picture of this little-known species.

Distribution, status and habitat conservation

This heron is found only on the island of New Guinea and a few off the larger islands off the west coast, and even then only in a few areas. It lives well inland along rivers with deep forest.

Feeding

The New Guinea Tiger Heron eats fish, crabs, aquatic insects, lizards and snakes.

Breeding

Only one stick nest, high up in a tree has ever been found. A single yellowish down chick was in the nest. No eggs have been seen.

Much like an immature bird, this tiger heron is now very rare indeed.

47

WHITE-CRESTED TIGER HERON

Tigriornis leucolophus

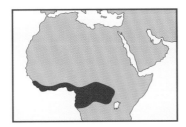

Since most of this rarely seen heron's habitat has been savagely fought over by marauding tribes, that it should have survived in any numbers at all is something of a miracle. Like its relative in New Guinea, this species is suitably plumaged to reflect the shadowy forests in which it lives. Its only decorative feature is the white crest from which it derives its name.

Identification

Length: 66–80 cm (26–32 in)

This, the only African member of the tiger heron family, is a darker speckled color than the New Guinea bird, but of a similar pattern. The deep buff color is heavily marked with black bars. The underparts are lighter with paler buff bars. The one distinguishing feature, from which it derives its name, is a quite long white crest below its black crest and nape. Its bill is dark horn and the lores green. The eye is dull yellow. The female has narrower buff barring above, and the underside is a dull pinkish color.

This species utters a bittern-like boom.

Distribution, status and habitat conservation

The White-crested Tiger Heron is found only in tropical African rainforests. It ranges from Sierra Leone and Liberia along the coast then south to the north of the Zaire River. From Gabon eastward to eastern Zaire, to some 200 km west (124 miles) of Lake Albert. Much of the habitat there, however, has been destroyed as it has over much of this bird's range.

It lives on small streams and swampy areas in heavy equatorial rainforest, and occasionally in tidal mangrove creeks. It must now be a most endangered species.

Feeding

Insects, frogs, snakes and fish are eaten by this heron.

Breeding

A captive bird spread its tail and crest in display and moved from side to side hissing the while. This was probably a threat display, but no more is known.

One nest has been found: this was a loose platform of twigs 6 m (20 feet) up a tree overhanging a dried out riverbed. It contained a single egg, that was beige-colored with large gray blotches and some red spots. The chick has yellow down which turns white and clings to the emerging feathers to give a bedraggled appearance.

This captive young was taken in Liberia. Only one nest of this species has been recorded.

Picture Credits

I thank those listed below for the many fine pictures, both photographs and portraits, used to supplement my own photography in this book.

Species photographs

Ted Below	- p. 71, p. 72 (top), p. 73 (below left).
Benjamin Busto	- Ch. 34, p.191 (below).
Peter Davey ARPS	- Ch. 31, Ch. 47.
Robert Gillmor	- Ch. 38, Ch. 39, Ch. 40, Ch. 41.
C. Clem Haagner/Photo Researchers	- p.80.
Peter Hayman	- Ch. 8, Ch. 9, Ch. 44, Ch. 46 , Ch. 47.
Andrew Henley/Nature Focus	- p.53.
Brenda J. Holcombe/Windrush	- p. 191 (above right).
Viesturs Klimpins/Latvian University	- p.17
Mike Lane/Aquila	- p. 81.
Dr C. Perrins	- p. 197 (above).
George Reszeter	- p. 127 (below)
Dave Richards FRPS	- Ch. 32.
David Tipling/Windrush	- Ch. 30.
Dr C.R. Tyler/Windrush	- p. 191 (above left).
James Walford	- p. 85 (below), Ch 36, p. 199 (above), p. 199 (below).
Gary Weber/Nature Focus	- p. 43, p. 98 (below)

INDEX

Page references in **bold** refer to the main discussion.

African Open-billed Storks 83
Agami Heron 9, **162–3**
Agamia agami see Agami Heron
Amaurornis flavirostra see Black Crake
Ardea sp. 8, 9, 144
Ardea cinerea 17
Ardea cinerea see Grey Heron
Ardea cinerea jouyi see Grey Heron
Ardea cinerea monicae see Grey Heron
Ardea cocoi see Cocoi Heron
Ardea goliath see Goliath Heron
Ardea herodius see Great Blue Heron
Ardea herodius fannini see Great Blue Heron
Ardea herodius occidentalis see Great Blue Heron
Ardea herodius wardii see Great Blue Heron
Ardea humbloti see Malagasy Heron
Ardea imperialis see Imperial Heron
Ardea melanocephala see Black-headed Heron
Ardea pacifica see White-necked Heron
Ardea purpurea see Purple Heron
Ardea purpurea madagascariensis see Purple Heron
Ardea purpurea manilensis see Purple Heron

Ardea sumatrana see Sumatran Heron
Ardeola sp. 9
Ardeola bacchus see Chinese Pond Heron
Ardeola grayii see Indian Pond Heron
Ardeola idea see Malagasy Pond Heron
Ardeola ralloides see Squacco Heron
Ardeola rufiventris see Rufous-bellied Heron
Ardeola speciosa see Javanese Pond Heron
Ardeomae 8

Bare-throated Tiger Heron **189–91**, 193
Black Crake 156
Black Heron 79, **82–5**
Black-crowned Night Heron 10, 166, **168–72**, 173, 174, 184
Black-headed Heron 8, 9, 20, **44–6**, 90
Black-winged Stilts 156
Boat-billed Heron **185–8**
Bubulcus sp. 9
Bubulcus ibis see Cattle Egret
Bubulcus ibis coromandus see Cattle Egret
Bubulcus ibis ibis see Cattle Egret
Bubulcus ibis seychellarum see Cattle Egret
Butorides striatus see Green-backed Heron

Butorides striatus atricapillus see Green-backed Heron
Butorides striatus immaculatus see Green-backed Heron
Butorides striatus stagnatalis see Green-backed Heron
Butorides striatus viviscens see Green-backed Heron

Capped Heron 8, **25–7**
Casmerodius 9
Cattle Egret 9, 20, **137–42**
Chinese Egret see Swinhoe's Egret
Chinese Pond Heron 9, **149–50**, 151
Cochlearius cochlearius see Boat-billed Heron
Cocoi Heron 8, **38–40**

Eastern Reef Heron 129, **131–6**
Egretta sp. 9, 42, 144
Egretta alba see Great White Egret
Egretta alba alba see Great White Egret
Egretta alba egretta see Great White Egret
Egretta alba melanorhyncos see Great White Egret
Egretta alba modesta see Great White Egret
Egretta ardesiaca see Black Heron
Egretta caerulea see Little Blue Heron
Egretta eulophotes see Swinhoe's Egret
Egretta garzetta see Little Egret
Egretta garzetta dimorpha see Little Egret
Egretta garzetta garzetta see Little Egret
Egretta garzetta gularis see Little Egret
Egretta garzetta immaculata see Little Egret
Egretta garzetta nigripes see Little Egret
Egretta garzetta schistacea see Little Egret
Egretta intermedia see Intermediate Egret

Egretta intermedia brachyryncha see Intermediate Egret
Egretta intermedia intermedia see Intermediate Egret
Egretta intermedia plumifera see Intermediate Egret
Egretta novaehollandiae see White-faced Heron
Egretta picata see Pied Heron
Egretta rufescens see Reddish Egret
Egretta sacra see Eastern Reef Heron
Egretta thula see Snowy Egret
Egretta thula brewsteri see Snowy Egret
Egretta tricolor see Tricolored Heron
Egretta tricolor ruficollis see Tricolored Heron
Egretta vinaceigula see Slaty Egret

Fasciated Tiger Heron **192–3**
Goliath Heron **55–8**
Gorsachius sp. 10
Gorsachius goisagi see Japanese Night Heron
Gorsachius magnificus see White-eared Night Heron
Gorsachius melanolopus see Malayan Night Heron
Great Blue Heron 8, 19, **32–7**, 38
Great White Egret 9, 17, 19, **64–9**, 90, 91
Green-backed Heron 7, 9, 11, 144, **157–61**
Grey Heron 7, 8, 17, **28–31**, 38, 59

Himantopus himantopus see Black-winged Stilts

Imperial Heron 8, **50–1**
Indian Pond Heron 9, **146–8**
Intermediate Egret 19, **90–5**

Japanese Night Heron **181–2**
Javanese Pond Heron 9, **151–2**

Little Blue Heron **99–103**, 110
Little Egret 8, 9, 17, 77, **108–27**, 131

Louisiana Heron see Tricolored Heron

Malagasy Pond Heron 8, 9, **47–9**, 50, 153–4
Malayan Night Heron **183–4**

Nankeen Night Heron 10, **173–5**
New Guinea Tiger Heron **201–2**
Nyctanassa violaceus see Yellow-crowned Night Heron
Nycticoracinae 8
Nycticorax sp. 10
Nycticorax caledonicus see Nankeen Night Heron
Nycticorax caledonicus hilli see Nankeen Night Heron
Nycticorax leuconotus see White-backed Night Heron
Nycticorax nycticorax see Black-crowned Night Heron
Nycticorax nycticorax hoactli see Black-crowned Night Heron
Nycticorax nycticorax nycticorae see Black-crowned Night Heron
Nycticorax violaceus see Yellow-crowned Night Heron
Nycticorax violaceus bancrofti see Yellow-crowned Night Heron
Nycticorax violaceus caliginis see Yellow-crowned Night Heron
Nycticorax violaceus cayennsis see Yellow-crowned Night Heron
Nycticorax violaceus pauper see Yellow-crowned Night Heron
Pied Egret 68
Pied Heron **74–8**
Pilherodius pileatus see Capped Heron
Plumed Egret 90, 93 *see also* Intermediate Egret
Purple Heron 17, **59–63**

Reddish Egret **70–3**, 86, 110
Rufescent Tiger Heron 10, 193, **194–200**

Rufous-bellied Heron 9, **155–6**

Scarlet Ibis 99
Slaty Egret **79–81**
Snowy Egret 9, 99, **104–7**
Squacco Heron 9, **143–5**, 153, 154, 156
Sumatran Heron **52–4**, 8
Swinhoe's Egret 110, **128–30**
Syrigma sibilatria see Whistling Heron
Syrigma sibilatria sibilatrix see Whistling Heron
Syrigma sililatria fostersmithi see Whistling Heron

Tigriornis sp. 10
Tigriornis leucolophus see White-crested Tiger Heron
Tigrisoma sp. 10
Tigrisoma fasciatum see Fasciated Tiger Heron
Tigrisoma lineatum see Rufescent Tiger Heron
Tigrisoma mexicanum see Bare-throated Tiger Heron
Tigrisomatinae 8
Tricolored Heron 9, **86–9**

Western Reef Heron see Little Egret
Whistling Heron 8, **21–4**, 25, 194, 195
White-backed Night Heron **176–7**
White-crested Tiger Heron **203–4**
White-eared Night Heron **178–80**
White-faced Heron **96–8**
White-necked Heron **41–3**

Yellow-billed Egret 90, 92
Yellow-crowned Night Heron 10, **164–7**

Zonerodius sp. 10
Zonerodius heliosylus see New Guinea